The Third
Perspective

The Third Perspective

Brave Expression in the Age of Intolerance

Africa Brooke

hachette
BOOKS

New York

Hachette Go, an imprint of Hachette Books
Hachette Book Group
1290 Avenue of the Americas
New York, NY 10104
HachetteGo.com
Facebook.com/HachetteGo
Instagram.com/HachetteGo

First Edition: May 2024

Published by Hachette Go, an imprint of Hachette Book Group, Inc. The
Hachette Go name and logo are trademarks of the Hachette Book Group.

The Hachette Speakers Bureau provides a wide range of authors for speaking events. To find
out more, go to hachettespeakersbureau.com or email HachetteSpeakers@hbgusa.com.

Hachette Go books may be purchased in bulk for business, educational, or
promotional use. For information, please contact your local bookseller or email the
Hachette Book Group Special Markets Department at Special.Markets@hbgusa.com.

The publisher is not responsible for websites (or their
content) that are not owned by the publisher.

Library of Congress Cataloging-in-Publication Data

Name: Brooke, Africa, author.
Title: The third perspective: brave expression in the age of intolerance / Africa Brooke.
Description: First edition. | New York: Go, Hachette Books, 2024.
Identifiers: LCCN 2024003732 | ISBN 9780306835377 (hardcover) |
ISBN 9780306835384 (trade paperback) | ISBN 9780306835391 (ebook)
Subjects: LCSH: Communication—Psychological aspects. | Interpersonal relations.
Classification: LCC BF637.C45 B75 2024 | DDC 153.6—dc23/eng/20240311
LC record available at https://lccn.loc.gov/2024003732

ISBNs: 978-0-306-83537-7 (hardcover); 978-0-306-83539-1 (ebook)

Printed in the United States of America

LSC-C

Printing 2, 2024

CONTENTS

Life is much more enjoyable when you live it as though you've already been canceled.

—Africa Brooke

Introduction

The Unchanged Human

I s there still room for us as human beings to stumble, fuck up, learn, and grow—*privately and publicly*—without the overwhelming pressure to be perfect? I got my answer to that question in January 2021 when I wrote the open letter that would change the course of my personal and professional life. This letter, which has been read and shared by over nineteen million people (and counting), was titled "Why I'm Leaving the Cult of Wokeness." If the title incites an unpleasant reaction within you and assumptions start rising to the surface, pause for a moment, stay with the unease, and continue reading. That's why you're here.

Around the time I wrote this letter, after a series of high-profile events, people all over the Western world were rightfully demanding greater awareness of racial injustice, discrimination, and sexual assault. As a Black woman, I agreed with many of the progressive values being championed, and I stand by them today. Equality. Bodily autonomy. Access to resources. Diversity. Yet something didn't feel quite right. Why was "diversity *of thought*" not being considered an important part of the equation?

I noticed an aversion to any questions or open discussions that brought up psychological discomfort, highlighted contradictions, or pointed out untruths. The biggest questions I had included: When we talk about social justice, are we considering the whole story of the past and the way people lived and thought back then, or are we judging yesterday based on today's beliefs in a way that might be too simple? Are we dismissing people too quickly if they don't share our views? Shouldn't we concentrate more on making things right and mending relationships, instead of putting all our energy into getting even and penalizing wrongs? By calling every differing opinion "problematic," aren't we risking missing out on important conversations that could challenge us to think differently? As the goalposts kept moving and more and more conversations continued to be shut down, even in spaces that were lauded as "safe," this restrictive way of engaging with the world was becoming somewhat of a distorted mirror.

Inside that mirror I saw a version of myself that made me very uneasy: an insufferable, self-righteous, self-proclaimed "ally" and "good person" who signaled her virtue noisily. I was in denial about the mismatch between what I was saying and what my behavior showed. I was saying that I wanted white people in America, Britain, and Europe to understand how different life is as a Black person existing on the margins of Western society. *Fair.* I was saying that I wanted men to grasp how society worked against women. *Fair.* I was *saying* that I wanted to create dialogues about these kinds of subjects. *Fair.* But I was not *listening* to anyone whose views failed to match my own. *Questionable.*

I was quick to judge, becoming close-minded toward others. I began to reject the idea that people can change their behavior (you'll think that is rich when you learn more about me in a moment). And it wasn't just me—well-meaning people all around me had become more intolerant of anyone not echoing their beliefs.

The year I wrote my open letter was the year I had to admit that my own fight against intolerance was marred by the fact that I'd become a physical representation of the intolerance I claimed to oppose. I had unknowingly neglected my innate curiosity, empathy, and understanding—especially when it meant understanding viewpoints that didn't align with my agenda. In my quest to be perceived as a "good" person, I had forgotten how to be a fully rounded human being, one who recognizes their own flaws as well as those of others.

This wasn't fun stuff to admit to, but I needed to be honest. I owed it to myself. Continually nodding along to ideas that no longer resonated with me was becoming draining. The oversimplification of intricate issues weighed heavily on my conscience. I rejected the idea that my skin color inherently labeled me oppressed, or that every white individual I encountered was prejudiced. I resisted buying into the narrative that cast men in a perpetual shadow of threat. I was sick of being told that I was doomed to victimhood. It dawned on me how much these beliefs had unknowingly caged my sense of agency. While I acknowledged that there's a spectrum of truths within these ideas, the strain of masking my true feelings with superficial agreement was reaching a breaking point.

It's evident to me now that my letter was an act of personal liberation, an attempt to soothe my nervous system and nurture my mental health. It was my hands-up moment. I couldn't play the game any longer. And if that made me a target for cancellation, I was more than willing to take the hit. This letter ended up serving as a permission slip for many others worldwide. Millions. It turns out, I wasn't the only one questioning what "virtuous people" were supposed to think. Others, too, felt trapped and unable to freely express their thoughts and opinions. My letter had started an important conversation.

If you'd heard of me before you bought this book, it was probably through social media. These days, most of my online sharing focuses on my widely known work, which I will detail, but, starting from 2016, my first years of public writing focused on my experiences with getting sober after a decade-long struggle with alcohol and other recreational drugs. This dance with my own darkness included seven spectacular relapses, fractured relationships, compulsive sexual behavior, a missing front tooth, cheating, manipulation, pathological lying, kleptomania, and an identity crisis from which I didn't expect to recover. That's as tidy as I can list it all.

These are messy, uncomfortable, ugly things that most of us hide from the world. But getting my shit together to make it past the age of twenty-four meant accepting responsibility for my disastrous life. No one was coming to save me.

After a lifetime of repressing the truest parts of myself, I wanted to know why we pull the plugs on ourselves and silence our voices out of fear of what others might think. It turned out there were specific terms to describe these phenomena: self-sabotage and self-censorship.

SELF-SABOTAGE VERSUS SELF-CENSORSHIP

Imagine you're the captain of your own ship, navigating the vast seas of life. Self-sabotage is like drilling holes in your boat while you're in the middle of the ocean. Instead of sailing smoothly toward your goals, you're constantly working against yourself, often without realizing it. It's the mysterious force that makes you procrastinate on an important project, doubt your own worth, or give up just before the finish line. This is exactly what I had done at many different times in my life. While the reasons behind these actions can be complex, as you'll discover as you move through the pages of this book, the result is clear: they prevent you from reaching your full potential.

Self-censorship, on the other hand, is when you silence your own voice and hold back thoughts, feelings, or knowledge out of fear, doubt, or the desire to fit in. Think of it as gagging yourself before anyone else has a chance to. This visual may be a little confronting, but it gives you an opportunity for raw introspection, doesn't it? It's avoiding certain topics in conversation, not standing up for your beliefs, or holding back a novel idea because you fear how others might react. Self-censorship is a subtle form of self-sabotage. While it may seem like you're protecting yourself from potential criticism or conflict, in reality, you're stifling your own growth and authenticity. Each time you censor yourself, you deny the world your unique perspective and rob yourself of genuine interactions. Just as drilling holes in your ship slows your journey, silencing your voice dims your presence in the world. The connection between the two concepts is what sealed my decision to make this my life's work.

WHO AM I?

Through a continuous process of looking inward, becoming a student of psychology, openly discussing my recovery, sharing even the darkest moments for accountability, and maintaining a sense of curiosity, I came to accept my newfound identity as a nondrinker. This path led me to a pivotal decision: to devote my career to understand why we often end up sabotaging ourselves, even as we strive for success.

Fast-forward over seven years, and my career has taken unexpected and fulfilling turns. I've become a consultant and mentor, helping a diverse range of people—from top-level executives, entrepreneurs, athletes, and artists to dedicated activists and educators. My clients come to me for help with things like getting past self-sabotage, freely and effectively sharing what they really think, and feeling braver in how they carry and express themselves. Together we tackle these and other challenges, such as:

- **Limiting Beliefs and Behaviors:** Paralyzing thoughts and habits, which leave them waiting for that elusive "perfect" moment before they take action or voice their opinions.
- **Comfort Zone Confinement:** Clinging to familiar patterns by avoiding situations where they might need to speak up, resulting in limited exposure and missed opportunities.

Each time you censor
yourself, you deny the world
your unique perspective
and rob yourself of
genuine interactions.

- **Public Speaking and Stage Fright:** The prospect of addressing an audience brings a surge of anxiety, be it the overwhelming grip of stage fright or the subtle nervousness of sharing thoughts in group discussions.
- **Comparison and Self-Worth Issues:** Constantly comparing themselves to peers or industry leaders, leading to feelings of inadequacy and thinking they have nothing unique to offer.
- **Debilitating Self-Talk:** Holding on to an internal dialogue that constantly undermines their self-worth, capabilities, or the value of their ideas. Beliefs such as "I'm not good enough," "Others know better," or "I don't have what it takes."
- **Fear of Exploration:** *This is a big one!* For many, there's a tangible hesitancy to try new things, share groundbreaking ideas, or state opinions due to an overarching fear of failure or criticism.

Do you see your own struggles reflected in these points? If so, this book will be the guide you need. With expertise in helping my clients overcome such hurdles, I'll be equipping you with cognitive strategies, communication skills, and emotional-intelligence training to help you break through these barriers and speak with confidence and clear intent even in moments when you are terrified. I've walked some of the most exceptional minds through the tough but rewarding path of transformation, a path where you quickly discover that real progress means facing discomfort head-on. With a wealth of diverse experience under my belt, I'm well-positioned to also guide you toward meaningful change. With my proven expertise and confidence, you can trust me to be a valuable asset in your journey.

HOW THIS BOOK CAN HELP YOU

As you dive into this book, you're signing up for more than just reading—you're stepping into an active training ground for your mind. You're not going to be playing safe; you will be making a commitment to *playing brave*. Together, we'll pinpoint, confront, and transform the twisted or negative thinking that's been silencing your authentic voice or bringing forward a voice that is not helping you. It's not just about thinking differently, it's about proving those old stories wrong through real-world challenges. This isn't simply a place to sit back and reflect; it's a place to stand up and act. You'll be documenting your journey and mapping out your mental shifts as you progress. To truly reap the benefits of this book, you need to engage with it, roll up your sleeves, and get your hands dirty. It's all about intentional action. Don't passively absorb the words—make them work for you. Your transformation demands your participation. There are exercises throughout for you to engage with, so grab a notebook, journal, pen, or digital device if you prefer typing, and have them handy as you work through each chapter.

This book is for you if societal pressures have been boxing in your thoughts and opinions, and you're eager to break free. If you've navigated through lost friendships, workplace disputes, or family disagreements over different beliefs or values, these pages will resonate with you. It's for those who crave real conversations where diverse viewpoints are not only accepted but appreciated. If, like me, you're done tiptoeing around sensitive topics but aren't sure about the next steps, this is your guide. Here, you'll learn to embrace thoughts and actions that go beyond simple black-and-white thinking. You'll pinpoint your core values, refine how you communicate and listen, clarify your intended messages, and determine what risks you're ready to take for your beliefs. And then, the real practice begins!

Though this book isn't an extended version of my open letter, I will not be shying away from addressing the difficult topics at hand. What you'll be reading is the result of me spending several years actively listening, researching, and concluding that we, as a society, have created a culture of fear—and people are desperate for nuance and open dialogue. People want to be treated as the complex, dynamic human beings they are. We deserve that. *You* deserve that. People like you are craving spaces where they can think and speak freely without being punished for it. This book is that space.

We're living in a time where contrasting views are swiftly dismissed. People are punished and disposed of if their opinions don't align with the popular narrative. A lot of my clients come to me because their personal *and* professional relationships are breaking under the pressure of ideologies and lack of patience. In a world where "Educate yourself!" has become a substitute for helping someone gain clarity on a topic, there's a growing desire for balance, empathy, and real-world solutions. An increasing amount of people are recognizing that narrow-mindedness is unsustainable. More of us are seeing that there is value in having difficult conversations. Some are even willing to face the realization that they, too, have behaved in ways that don't align with their true values. Perhaps you're one of those people. And I'm telling you now, that's fine. This is your route to step back and reevaluate, free from any shame.

Whether you're speaking with your client, colleague, business partner, employee, boss, spouse, child, grandparent, doctor, friend, acquaintance, or a stranger in the supermarket, you'll be equipped to share your views, hear theirs, make a point you feel must be made, and move on with your day feeling honest, open, and true to yourself. Hopefully without losing your shit. You'll learn that bold, uncomfortable discussions are a must. So is humor, play, and a willingness to laugh at your own absurdity. That's what I'm here to remind us. Never take yourself too seriously . . . at least not all the time.

As you begin to understand and enjoy your own complexity, you'll feel a profound shift in your interactions with others. You'll find yourself approaching conversations with curiosity, rather than judgment. You'll appreciate diversity in thoughts and opinions, instead of seeing them as threats to your own beliefs or feeling the pressure to agree. You'll find comfort in uncertainty, knowing that it's a pathway to growth and understanding, rather than a source of fear and confusion. All of this, including the challenging stuff, is good news. Making these changes requires work, but it puts you back in the driver's seat, reactivates your courage, builds your emotional resilience, and allows you to move forward in the direction you want, instead of being at the mercy of the external world.

WHAT IS "THE THIRD PERSPECTIVE"?

"The Third Perspective" is more than a concept. I want you to think of it as a return to that part of your mind where spaciousness, tranquility, curiosity, openness, and understanding live. It's a tool for breaking free from the limitations of echo chambers and self-imposed restrictions.

This perspective is powerful. It's your ally in resisting the urge to self-police your thoughts, to stop betraying yourself in sneaky ways for the sake of appearing "good," and to move beyond constrained thinking. By the end of this book, you'll be able to use it in various aspects of life:

- **Conflict Resolution:** Rather than clinging to one viewpoint or caving to another, you'll strive for solutions that respect both sides or find a middle way.
- **Negotiation:** You'll shift from a "win–lose" to a "win–win" mindset, creating outcomes that are fulfilling for everyone involved.
- **Voting:** You'll move beyond rigid party loyalty; weigh up individual policies and their broader impacts.
- **Decision-Making:** When stuck between two choices, you'll think outside the box. You'll remember that there might be a third, more advantageous, option waiting to be discovered.

- **Life Balance:** You'll look for ways to blend your passions with your work, seeking harmony rather than a strict separation of work and play.
- **Creative Endeavors:** Don't limit yourself to one style or genre. You'll experiment by blending elements from different areas to forge something truly unique.
- **Discussing Controversial Topics:** When faced with polarizing issues, you'll resist the urge to align unwaveringly with one side. Instead, you can delve into the nuances and complexities to gain a more rounded understanding of the matter.

Each of these applications of The Third Perspective opens up new paths for thinking and living, inviting more meaningful and satisfying experiences into your life.

This book is designed to support you in returning to life's rich complexity—which includes being rooted in the realization that people contain multitudes and can surprise you, especially when offered the grace to reveal themselves. Embracing this understanding is central to our focus, as it's a crucial element in bravely expressing yourself in an era often marked by intolerance. If you're already thinking, "Well, good for *you* for being open-minded, but I won't be tolerating bigots…," then you're in for a pleasant surprise.

The Third Perspective will serve as a reminder that understanding isn't synonymous with acceptance. I will not be teaching you to blindly accept everyone's opinions, but to forge mutual respect and connection in an environment where all voices can be heard. Curiosity about someone's reasoning doesn't equate to agreement—you will learn that here. You will also learn that discernment is your friend. I won't be asking you to compromise your boundaries and principles. Far from it. Instead, my aim is to help you check in on those boundaries to make sure they are not actually walls. I want you to handle yourself confidently and effectively when you are confronted with information or people you disagree with, and especially when you engage in challenging conversations.

I won't be dictating a path for you or presenting you with a rule-book. What I will give you is an opportunity to create a road map that has the power to transform your relationship with yourself, the people around you, and the world at large. It's an invitation for dialogue and self-actualization.

My promise is that you will change the way you interact with other people so that you are relaxed in discussing your beliefs, thoughts, and feelings—especially when those you're facing don't agree with you. Our work will allow you to enter any potentially difficult discussion about politics, society, personal responsibility, duty, race, sex, gender, or religion while remaining calm and comfortable with who you are.

I don't mean that you'll have all the answers on every topic. I know *I* don't have them. I mean you will be able to explain your thoughts and reserve the right to disagree with others, even when you don't have the solution yourself. Nor am I promising to turn you into a keyboard warrior, so certain in your views and approach that you can take on the comment section single-handedly. If that's your ambition, this book will likely be helpful to you, but I'll be asking you to rethink your life choices.

DISCLAIMER

Maybe don't read this book if you're looking for a solution that won't involve effort and getting uncomfortable. I'm asking you to commit to a practical process that requires active integration of what you learn here. You won't magically change into someone braver and freer just by reading a book. But if you are willing to stay curious and risk being a little scared, I believe you'll get more than you hoped for.

You will change the way you interact with other people so that you are relaxed in discussing your beliefs, thoughts, and feelings— especially when those you're facing don't agree with you.

If you'd like to stop worrying about whether other people will disagree with you, then it's important that I tell you now: those worries and communication blocks are not going to magically resolve themselves. You must be willing to get your ass into the arena and test out different ways of communicating. You must understand the difference between silencing yourself out of fear, "reading the room," and judging each situation carefully.

If you love holding people hostage with your beliefs and opinions, you might think I'm about to tell you to not bother turning the page, but you're top of my reader wish list. The same applies if you think that anyone who doesn't vote for your political party is, at best, stupid, most probably a "scumbag," and quite possibly evil. If you believe that this is not your problem and you pretty much always know what's right and what's wrong, let's put that to the test. I truly believe that if you walk this path in good faith, the impact will be life-changing.

Are you ready to begin reclaiming independent thought? Are you ready to clear out the groupthink that has penetrated your worldview? Are you ready to *refine* your own worldview? If you answered YES to any of these questions, you are in the right place.

THE THREE PILLARS

In my private practice, and within my online communities, I speak to hundreds of people each week who are breaking out of their mind prisons and echo chambers. People are increasingly open about their wish to engage with the world in a grounded and thoughtful way. *The Third Perspective* will provide you with a framework to do exactly that. Split into three parts, pillars if you will—Awareness, Responsibility, and Expression—this book will explore the all-important questions: *What are you afraid of, what do you stand for,* and *what are you willing to risk?* The answers to each of these questions will be as unique as your fingerprint.

The first pillar of Awareness explores *honest introspection*: a willingness to look your own BS in the eye—and befriend it. It's time to face the messier parts of your thoughts and feelings head-on, like meeting an old frenemy. You're not just going to look at what's wrong out there in the world; you're going to take a good, hard look at what's going on inside you, too. It's a lot easier to blame the world for being unfair, but if you want to make a real difference, you've got to start with yourself. But you knew that, right? We're quick to call out others, but the hardest part is spotting our own hidden biases and fears. I'll be right there with you, helping you tell the difference between when you're holding back out of fear and when you're choosing to stay quiet wisely. Together, we'll uncover the fears and superstitions you've tucked away. Spot them, understand them, and get ready to change the narrative. Once you see what you're really dealing with, you can start fixing it.

The second pillar of Responsibility asks you to *create your personal philosophy*: we'll take a deep dive into what makes you, well, YOU. When the going gets tough, can you stand firm, wear your values on your sleeve, and champion them? And before we get ahead of ourselves, can you even *list* them? This segment is all about fine-tuning those core beliefs and values. You'll also make sure that your communication style—the way you convey these beliefs to the world—serves you. Is your communication style a trustworthy friend or is it sneakily undermining you? Together, we'll refine and perfect this, ensuring you're not just heard, but genuinely understood.

Finally, in Expression, you will practice *honing your voice mind-fully*: it's all about sharpening *how* you speak your mind. It's one thing to find your voice, but another to use it deliberately (with purpose and precision), shaped by everything you've reflected on. You'll learn to activate the maverick within you and clear the everyday communication blocks that trip up most of us. But the true game changer? Pinpointing the risks you're ready to take for the sake of saying what you truly mean. This is about making sure your voice stays strong, no matter who's listening. And it's not just about what you say—your body language speaks volumes, too. You'll learn to use that to add more meaning to your words. By the end of this pillar, armed with insights and empowered by practice, you'll be ready for the most exciting part of it all: the reintroduction you will make to announce who you are *becoming*. You will find your own truth, harness the courage to express it, and step into the world with a brave (and effective) voice in tow.

As we tackle each pillar of this journey, I'll show you how thinking for yourself, asking tough questions, and bouncing back from emotional knocks are key to dealing with the lack of tolerance we see around us—and the kind we have inside us, too. You'll challenge what you've always thought was true, give your opinions a second look, and get better at talking and connecting with people in a way that's honest and works. You'll learn to break free from the "it's this or that" way of thinking that keeps us from being truly inclusive.

Think of The Third Perspective framework like a trusted friend who's there to guide you as you start asking the big questions, looking at things differently, and growing from what you find. It's a method I've spent years developing and using to successfully help thousands of people move from self-censorship into speaking their minds thoughtfully. This process works, and if you're ready to put in the effort with me, you will experience its transformative gifts—even if you are skeptical.

Inside this book, you'll learn how your own ideas and voice matter—not just for you, but for everyone in the world. For our global community. Yes, I'm convinced we can get back to having real, meaningful conversations without losing our connections with each other. You'll play a big part in creating our shared story—a story that's as rich, varied, and wonderful as we, its authors, allow it to be. This book is going to be a key part of your journey to live a life filled with meaning, honesty, happiness, a good sense of humor, and just the right amount of audacity. It will arm you with fresh confidence when faced with some of the worst aspects of today's world. Remember: every conversation, every interaction, every thought, every decision is an opportunity to apply The Third Perspective.

They have their story. You have yours. And somewhere in the in-between, in the nuances and the subtleties, lies *your* Third Perspective—your undiscovered catalyst and springboard for change. Now, let's begin.

The Third Perspective

PART 1

Awareness:

WHAT ARE YOU AFRAID OF?

W elcome to the start of your self-awakening.

In the opening chapters of this book, you'll explore how the noise of self-doubt, fear, and self-judgment can crowd your mind and cause you to sabotage yourself. Think of this as meeting an inner mob, each voice clamoring for your attention, often drowning out reason with fear. Change happens in the mind first, so this is where we will begin. We're going to get to know these noisy thoughts better, not to pick a fight, but to make peace with them. This will be a foundational first step before you look at how today's "cancel culture"— what I call "collective sabotage"—can make you scared to say what you really think. Understanding this will help you see why sometimes you might choose to stay quiet instead of speaking up, even if you consider yourself to be a confident and outspoken person. By identifying whether you are in the stifling grip of self-censorship—being overly cautious and silencing every word before it leaves your lips—or the unchecked abandon of an unrefined social filter—lacking nuance and shouting every thought without discretion—*or perhaps somewhere in the middle*, you'll be poised to communicate not just loudly, but wisely and effectively.

And we can't ignore social media—it has a big say in why we might hide our true thoughts. We'll figure out how you're using it: Are you holding your words back too much or are you saying everything

3

without thinking it through? By figuring out where you stand, you'll learn to find a middle ground, so your voice is clear, smart, and gets through to people in the way you intend it to.

This first pillar will bring to light all the things that you might not have considered, and, through it all, I'll be here to help you find balance. This introspection might not be easy, but it'll be worth it. You may uncover things about yourself that you've been avoiding, but remember, acceptance is the first step toward change. You have to *understand* the environment to be *effective* in the environment. Together, we'll reveal any underlying fears or resistance, and forge your road map to brave expression. We will make sure you're not merely a voice in the wilderness, but a voice of reason, clarity, and impact. Let's turn on the lights and illuminate the parts of you that have been holding you back.

Chapter 1

Conformity Is Not the Answer

Think of a government censoring the press, a movie being edited before release because of concerns from the film board, or a book being pulled before (or even after) publication because of public outrage. When I was working in advertising years ago, this is something I witnessed on a regular basis. This is an example of censorship. It's a tangible, often visible, force and it imposes specific guidelines or rules about what can be said, broadcast, or published. I know that when we think of the word "censorship," we typically focus on what's happening outside of us like this. Self-censorship, on the other hand, is much more subtle—it comes from within. No one is directly telling you to stop or to change what you're saying. You're taking on the job yourself.

As you start turning inward and settling into a state of Awareness, I want you to imagine a world where every word, every belief, and every idea is under a microscope—watched closely and then picked apart. A world where conversations at dinner become quiet chats and it feels like you're always on edge, trying not to upset anyone. Every time you post online, you worry, "Will this get me lots of likes or a ton of angry comments?" This is a world most of us have become intimately familiar with—a world where we're all afraid of saying the wrong thing. Because of this fear, a lot of us are holding back. We're scared of being misunderstood, labeled, or left out. So we play it safe, not asking tough questions or speaking our minds. We're avoiding getting our feelings hurt, so we take fewer and fewer risks. We choose self-censorship over brave expression. Well, if you're reading these words, I'm here to tell you that it's time to opt out of playing that game.

Deep down, we all just want to share our thoughts, feelings, and beliefs freely. But with all the worry and judgment out there, it's tough figuring out the best way and time to open up about who we really are. Some of us are super cautious, afraid of saying the wrong thing. Others let everything out, sometimes without thinking of the impact. Finding that middle ground—that Third Perspective—where we can be true to ourselves, but also kind and considerate, that's the challenge of our times. It's the challenge we're here to face.

It's easy to agree that we want to think and speak more freely. It's harder to do it in a way that works for us and allows us to remain effective in the world. I know how uncomfortable it can be to announce to all the people around you that you disagree with their understanding of the ideas and the facts that mean most to them— and to you. I'm also aware that we tend to think of these problems as modern issues, a consequence of some new intolerance that's sprung up, but this line of thinking doesn't get to the core of the psychological and social realities that have created the situation. People have dreaded speaking their mind at most periods in history.

In ancient or modern tyrannies, people are right to be afraid— terrified—of criticizing their rulers and the ruling orthodoxy. You don't speak up without consequence today in Russia, Saudi Arabia, Zimbabwe (my home country), and a hundred other places.

The threat of dissent isn't usually life-threatening in a modern democracy, but it's easy to understand why we don't stand up for our beliefs. Today, a single social media post can receive an unimaginable number of likes or provoke a storm. Online platforms, which we'll explore in great detail later, while giving us a voice, have also amplified the weight of each word we share. All of which contributes to the self-silencing that fascinates and terrifies me so much.

No one wants to be ostracized, jeered, attacked, or shamed. But that doesn't make self-silencing the right choice for you. You erode your identity. You limit your development. If enough of us remain silent, we risk letting the values of debate, disagreement, and mutual respect be diminished. We contribute to the destruction of our world. We erode our identity. We limit our development.

It's become far too normalized to muzzle our words, second-guess our thoughts, and limit our expressiveness, even around those closest to us, which I personally believe is enough reason for sounding the alarm. Are you not supposed to feel safe enough to explore your wild ideas and thoughts with the people closest to you? This rigid climate is not only dictating our spoken words, it is shaping how we make art, how we form relationships, and even how we make day-to-day decisions. It is shaping our life choices.

THE BIOLOGY OF CONFORMITY

Let's take a little trip back in time. Our ancient ancestors lived in groups and relied on each other to survive. Getting kicked out of the group or being the odd one out? That was dangerous. So, fitting in and avoiding conflict was pretty much wired into our system. This wasn't about being weak or not standing up for oneself; it was about survival.

Fast-forward to today and, while we're not fending off wild animals or hunting for our next meal, our brains are still wired in a similar way. Deep down, we're cautious because we want to belong. We fear isolation, judgment, and conflict. That's why the thought of negative consequences from expressing an unpopular opinion can lead to that all-too-familiar feeling in the pit of your stomach. While writing this, I was taken back to my childhood as a young fourteen-year-old girl in school. I remember one summer coming back to school after the break and feeling a sense of discomfort within my body as I was walking through the school's campus. I wasn't quite sure why I felt this icky feeling, but I would soon find out.

I went to my classes as usual in the morning and I remember looking for my group of friends at lunchtime. They were nowhere to be seen. I still couldn't shake that heavy feeling in my chest, even though I had nothing to attach it to. Everything had been fine when I last saw everyone six weeks ago. I had been in touch with a couple of girls from the group over the break, so why did I feel so strange coming back to school that day? Why did I feel extremely anxious? Why did I feel like I was in trouble?

Finally, I found my friends in the cafeteria. This was the same group of girls that I had been spending time with for the past year. I quickly learned that they were not talking to me, but no one would tell me why I was suddenly outcast. I had done something but I wasn't allowed to know what it was. All I knew was that I was no longer part of the tribe. That rejection was my first heartbreak, and months later I would learn that I was pushed out of the circle because our group leader had heard a rumor that I liked the same boy she did.

As children, our school environment is usually our first experience of society outside of the family unit. It's where we first grapple with hierarchy outside of the home: the popular kids, the bullies, the quiet ones, and so on. It's the universe of first friendships, first betrayals, and the first tastes of group dynamics. School is where I first got to truly understand the unpredictable nature of human interactions. One day you're in, the next you're out. The "rules" are ever-changing and often unwritten. Breaking them, even unknowingly, can lead to harsh consequences. Sound familiar?

In situations like this, especially in an environment like school, your brain tries to make sense of things and often goes into self-preservation mode. You start tiptoeing around your friends and stifling your authentic self to avoid further rejection. The irony here is that you're essentially self-censoring in an environment where you're supposed to be learning and growing.

We don't tend to make the connection easily, but school experiences like mine create foundational patterns in our lives. They teach us about trust, loyalty, and the fine line between fitting in and standing out. Many of us carry the echoes of these lessons into adulthood, affecting how we navigate our professional and personal spaces. And while the cafeteria tables and school uniforms may be long behind you, the primal feelings they evoked—the need for acceptance, the fear of rejection—still linger.

These memories serve as vivid reminders that our reactions to fear, conformity, and self-censorship aren't just about biology or ancient evolutionary instincts. They're deeply personal, molded by experiences that struck a chord when we were young and impressionable. And it's not just about the playground; your early family life has a big part in it too. Go back to your formative years and think about how things were at home when you were growing up. Did your family talk openly about everything or was it more about not rocking the boat? Mine, as much as I love them, were more of the latter. These early experiences teach you when to speak, when to hold back, and, sometimes, when to hide your true thoughts and feelings. You learn early on whether it's okay to share your inner world or if it's better to just keep things to yourself. Understanding these early life lessons is important for figuring out why you self-censor and how you can start being more open about how you actually see and experience the world around you.

It's time to start rolling up those sleeves like you said you would. I created the following exercise to help you reflect on those early, formative experiences that have shaped you. Think back to your childhood and teen years—the playground politics, the dinner table dynamics, the silent rules of your community. Let's now explore how these experiences have molded your trust in others, your struggle between fitting in, standing out and being yourself, your pursuit of acceptance, and

If enough of us remain
silent, we risk letting
the values of debate,
disagreement, and mutual
respect be diminished.

your reactions to rejection. These aren't just distant memories; they're the building blocks of who you are today. By examining them, you're going to reveal patterns that still play out in your life, influencing your relationships and decisions, both personally and professionally. So, find a quiet spot and let's start going back in time. Be bold, be honest, and, most importantly, be open to the revelations that await. Don't judge them, shoo them away, or try to change them. Simply make note of what you find. This isn't just about looking back; it's about understanding and shaping who you become moving forward.

REFLECTING ON YOUR FORMATIVE EXPERIENCES

- **Trust and Betrayal:** Think back to a moment in your childhood or adolescence when someone broke your trust in a big way. Maybe a friend spilled a secret or a family member let you down. How has that moment shaped the way you trust (or don't trust) people now? Do you find yourself holding back, wary of giving your trust too easily?

- **The Tug-of-War Between Fitting In and Standing Out:** Reflect on those times when you felt torn between blending in with the crowd and showing your true colors. How did you navigate this struggle? Fast-forward to today: Do these battles still wage within you in your current life, and how specifically do they show up?

- **The Quest for Acceptance:** Consider the lengths you went to be accepted in your childhood or teenage years. None of us should get stuck on this one! Did you change your appearance, suppress your interests, or even partake in something you regret? Now, look at your life today. Are you still dancing to a similar tune, altering parts of yourself to fit in? No judgment here—lay it all out.

- **The Sting of Rejection:** Think back to a time when you felt deeply excluded or rejected. It could have been not getting

---

invited to a party or being picked last for a team. How do those raw, often painful, memories echo in your life now? Do they still influence how you interact with others or how you approach new relationships?

- **Navigating Life's Spaces:** How do these early experiences play out in your adult life, especially in professional or personal settings? Do you find yourself acting out old scripts in new environments? Are you repeating the same patterns, or have you learned to navigate differently?

This exercise is more than a trip down memory lane. You're taking a close look at the roots of your behaviors and beliefs. The insights you'll find here are incredibly valuable. Think of this exercise as the building block of your present and the road map to your future. It allows you to take stock of where you've been, where you are, and where you're headed. Remember, the goal at this stage isn't to immediately change or fix anything. It's about awareness, about taking an honest inventory of your life experiences. This awareness will be a guiding light as you travel through the rest of the book.

BRAIN TALK: WHAT'S HAPPENING UP THERE?

When faced with potential conflict or backlash, our brain's alarm system—the amygdala—goes off. It's like an internal alert, telling us, "Hey, this might be risky!" It goes beyond physical threats. Social threats, like feeling rejected or misunderstood, can spark similar reactions. It's exactly what I felt that afternoon in the cafeteria when I was told by my friends that I was no longer one of them, and I had no right to know why. I wanted to push back, defend myself, and tell them they were wrong about whatever my supposed sin was, but I was also scared that if I protested too much, I might be challenged to a physical fight. Oh, the joys of being a high schooler!

In situations where we fear judgment, backlash, or physical harm our brain releases stress hormones, like cortisol. Ever felt your heart race, your palms get sweaty, or your stomach tighten when you're about to say something controversial? Yep, that's your body responding to that internal alert. On the flip side, when we choose to self-censor and avoid potential conflict, it might feel like a relief. That's because our brain rewards us with feel-good chemicals, like dopamine, when we avoid those perceived threats.

But here's the twist...

While our biological instincts push us to avoid conflict and fit in, we also have another part of our brain—the prefrontal cortex—that deals with reasoning, decision-making, and social interactions. It helps us weigh the pros and cons and decide if speaking up is worth the potential backlash. This is where our capacity for discernment-led social filtering comes in.

ARE YOU SELF-CENSORING OR USING A SOCIAL FILTER?

We touched on self-censorship in the Introduction, but to ensure this book sets you up for success, I need to give some more context on what the hell I'm talking about. What is self-censorship, and why should you care? Well, it's not a term that we think about when we're getting on with our day, when we're having conversations with our friends, or when we're wondering what that feeling of anxiety is in our chest, but you've probably practiced it more times than you can count. I'm no exception to this. At its core, self-censorship is the act of holding back your honest thoughts and feelings because you are anticipating something bad happening as a result. Think of it as that voice inside your head cautioning, "Better not say that." It's the decision your "inner protector" makes to not voice a thought, not because it's wrong or baseless, but because expressing it might lead to a blowback or misrepresentation. It's that second-guessing, that internal tug-of-war between speaking out and staying silent.

How often have you tamed your thoughts and diluted your opinions? Have you found yourself hesitating before discussing a musician who's suddenly not the darling of the public anymore? I know I have. When you come across a heated debate on social media about a previously adored author who's now facing waves of online criticism, do you feel the pull to join in or does caution keep you scrolling past? Do you find yourself wondering if you are a "bad person" because you maybe agree with the view everyone is pushing back against? And when you think of sharing an opinion or simply asking a question on touchy subjects like immigration, LGBTQ+ rights, or choices in parenting, do you often pause, weighing the worth of your voice against the potential fallout? And when *is* that pausing or silence simply a practice in discernment? You'll soon find out.

External censorship would be like the religious authorities in Renaissance Europe explicitly telling writers what they can or cannot write. Meanwhile, self-censorship is more akin to historians in ancient China choosing on their own to leave out certain events. In today's digital age, the lines can blur. The threat of being ripped to shreds for speaking your mind might push you to silence yourself even if there's no direct authority dictating the silence.

On the flip side, there are some of us who just blurt out whatever's on our mind without thinking, without considering how it might come across. In trying to be bold or honest, we might end up causing more problems, rubbing people the wrong way, or stirring the pot without meaning to. Sometimes, we get so caught up in being honest that it can backfire. Like when you quickly post something bold on social media and then get a bunch of angry replies. Or when, in the interest of being direct, you shoot down a coworker's idea too fast, thinking you're just getting to the point. Or when you're so passionate about something at dinner, only to realize that you've silenced the whole table and nobody else got a word in. Being direct is great—we want more of that—but if we're not more careful and understanding, what we're trying to say can get muddled and come out all wrong.

My clients tend to be people who fit both descriptions, and I always tell them that both extremes—holding back out of fear and speaking impulsively without filtering—show just how tricky it can be to express ourselves.

For years now I've been wondering what the solution is to this collective problem. Perhaps you've been wondering about this, too, and maybe it's why you picked up this book. I don't for a second believe that I have the one answer that will solve the world's problems, but I do think there is more within our control than we realize.

Saying *everything* and saying *nothing* are not your only options, even if our binary-loving brain would rather have us believe we only ever have two choices. You have a host of thoughts, opinions, jokes, and stories at your disposal. How you choose to share these thoughts, and which ones you decide to keep to yourself, essentially showcases the difference between self-censorship and using a social filter—a brilliant thinking skill that allows you to "read the room." Your social filter is the brain filter there to remind you that telling your lovely eccentric aunt that her new pixie haircut looks a bit like Ed Sheeran's messy hair is not the wisest or kindest idea.

I like to think of using a social filter as being like sorting through your wardrobe to pick the right outfit for a specific occasion. You're making conscious decisions about what to say, considering the social setting, the people around you, and the potential impact of your words. You might skip telling a particularly crude joke because you're aware it could offend someone present, but you may be able to tell that exact same joke with a couple of friends because you know that it'll land in the way you want it to. That's not you being afraid, that's you being considerate. You're adapting your communication to suit the setting. This is discernment-led behavior, rooted in understanding and empathy. As someone who loves a crude joke every now and again, believe me, there really is a time and a place. On the other hand, self-censorship is less like picking an outfit and more like not going to the party at all because you're afraid your

Saying *everything* and saying *nothing* are not your only options.

clothes won't be good enough. It's fear-driven. You might have an opinion or a story you'd like to share, but you keep quiet because you're afraid of the potential backlash or ridicule. You're worried about how others may perceive you, or how their perception might affect your social standing, job security, or legal standing in extreme cases. This self-censorship can leave you feeling suppressed, unheard, or unseen.

So, the next time you find yourself deciding whether to speak or stay silent, consider if you're choosing the right outfit for the party, or if you're too scared to attend the party at all.

THE DIFFERENCE

Not speaking out of fear (self-censoring):
- **Why?** Afraid of what might happen.
- **What's Held Back?** Real thoughts or feelings.
- **Whose Rules?** Society's or some group's expectations.
- **Talking Quality?** Not many different views, lots of holding back.
- **How's It Come About?** A quick, defensive reaction.
- **How's It Feel?** Leaves you uneasy, upset, or unsatisfied.
- **Growth?** Hard to learn new things when you're not hearing different ideas.

Choosing words wisely (social filtering):
- **Why?** Thinking about the situation and who you're talking to.
- **What's Said?** Honest words, chosen carefully.
- **Whose Rules?** Your own values and understanding.
- **Talking Quality?** Good conversations that consider others' feelings.
- **How's It Come About?** Thinking ahead and understanding.
- **How's It Feel?** Like you're true to yourself and respectful of others.
- **Growth?** Great conversations that respect limits and recognize differences.

THE ROLE OF FEAR

Often, it's fear that pushes us to silence ourselves. Any time that I've stopped myself from being honest about what was in my heart and mind, it was because of the fear of being judged, of showing my true self, or of conflict. It's like trying to sail smoothly through life's challenges without making waves. But sometimes, this strategy can make us lose touch with who we really are. A lot of the time, it just doesn't work.

Fear comes in many shapes: fear of what others think, fear of the unknown, fear of failure, and even fear of facing our own imperfections. This can lead to denial, where we put on a mask to avoid facing those fears. The relationship between fear and denial is complex, but understanding it can help us break free from patterns that might not serve us well.

Let me paint you a picture from an unsavory chapter in my own life. It's a tale of how the terrifying grip of fear can lead us down a twisted path of denial, of how even when the world screams the truth at us, we might choose to throw on noise-canceling headphones.

MY STORY

One summer I woke up to a faint yet familiar throbbing between my legs. A sign that I'd had sex, or at the very least been penetrated with something. Although I wasn't sure of the exact details, what I did know, based on previous experiences, was that I'd need to spend money I didn't have to buy a morning-after pill on the way home.

The last partial memory I had was of finishing a boozy lunch with a friend, then moving on to some seedy yet lively basement bar in central London. With this piece of information, along with texts sent and calls I'd made, I could try figuring out how I got from the bar and into the bed I found myself in. That's how I usually tracked my lost time—a personal game of CSI. The good news was that I was alive, seemingly unmarked and lying on what felt like a comfortable mattress. But where was I? I had no idea.

I'd binge-drunk my way into another blackout, again.

Between the ages of fourteen and twenty-four, I was an alcoholic. A blackout drinker. As adolescence transitioned into adulthood, drinking to the point of memory loss became more than just an escape, it became a ritual. My drinking didn't only pull out the worst in me; it shone a bright spotlight on it. It unleashed behaviors and traits that were far from flattering. I tried my best to keep this messy side hidden from myself and away from prying eyes, but it was a losing battle. Compulsive lying, kleptomania, and cheating on partners…these were just the top picks from a long, regrettable, and very ugly list.

Despite knowing the dangers that came with blackout drinking—vulnerability to predatory men, mental breakdown, and physical injury among them—I stubbornly held on, hell-bent on pushing the boundaries of my mind and body. The evidence showing me my life was falling apart was not enough to stop me from drinking and snorting my way through London.

My self-deception told me I needed alcohol to feel desirable, fuckable, to command attention, to be witty and charming, essentially promising liberation in every emptied glass. Denying the truth of my reality and silencing the increasingly loud inner voice that told me I had a serious problem made me feel like I was in control of my declining self-esteem. It helped minimize the guilt, but, most of all, the shame. Like most people, I used denial to create a positive and consistent self-concept in my mind.

As this lie grew, so did the distance between me and my family, despite us living under the same roof. They were fast becoming aware of my not-so-secret drinking habits, and their disapproval permeated the walls of our home. My personal relationships and work life teetered on the brink of collapse. Despite the turmoil and chaos, I clung to the belief that my drinking was not "that bad." At this point in my life, I could not and *would not* even consider that there might be another way, that something had to give. There was no "Third Perspective." Besides, it was *only* sporadic blackouts, not daily indulgence, right?

My internet search history was filled with: "Is it normal to lose your memory when you drink too much alcohol?" "How do you drink less alcohol without stopping completely?" "Signs you have a drinking problem," and so on. All the classics. At times, moderation worked, but it mostly didn't. For someone like me, moderating felt like pointless torture. Plus, the times when it worked became convenient excuses for why my so-called problem wasn't "so bad" after all.

After years of dodging the truth, my life brimming with proof of booze wreaking havoc, I could no longer ignore it. Maybe I was lucky in being forced to confront my own denial so young. Mine was a severe case that could have killed me quickly. I had to reluctantly confront the well-trained demons of my addiction and hold myself accountable for my actions without feeling entitled to forgiveness or understanding. Sobriety meant acknowledging that some people would always perceive me through the lens of their past experiences with me. It meant surrendering to reality—which will be a recurring theme in this book.

Seven grand relapses later, on November 7, 2016, I mustered the courage to try sobriety one more time. With nowhere else to turn, I chose to share my journey anonymously on Instagram. From my very first post, my chaotic life as a twenty-four-year-old binge drinker seeking help felt more manageable. I shared my fear of not reaching my twenty-fifth birthday if I didn't change my ways. I strived to be as open as my shame would allow, doing my best to depict my reality without glossing over my imperfections. That became my motto: always speak the *truth*, especially when it's easier to hide behind a lie.

While my story, drenched in denial, has its unique flavors, there's a universal undercurrent that ties it all together: *fear*. You see, fear isn't just about the immediate, tangible threats; it's about the inner monsters that gnaw at your self-worth, pushing you further into a vortex of denial, silencing your truths, and forcing you to act in ways that sabotage your essence. It's that trepidation that makes you bury your head in the sand or, in my case, at the bottom of a glass, regardless of the clear evidence around you.

REFLECTIVE QUESTIONS

Pause for a moment and ask yourself: What am I most afraid of? Is it judgment, failure, or perhaps admitting imperfections? Fear isn't just about the tangible threats you can touch or see; it often dwells deeper, affecting how you perceive yourself and the narratives you construct about your life.

The fear of admitting you're flawed, the fear of societal judgment, the fear of not being enough—all these can shape your choices, chaining you to patterns of behavior that seem impossible to break. For me, it took shape as an overpowering need to drown my sorrows and imperfections in alcohol. But what form does your fear take? Perhaps it's not a bottle, but a particular habit, a mask you wear, or a secret you bury deep within. Is there a pattern in your life you recognize but can't explain? Is there a behavior you justify despite knowing its harms? What truths are you possibly running from? It's these introspections that will help peel back the layers, exposing the rawness underneath.

But let's be real: it's not just my story. Many of us have our versions of blackouts, our shields of denial, built atop foundations of fear. It's what drives us to mask our genuine emotions, to put on facades, to choose paths that lead us further away from our true selves. Whether it's about personal relationships, professional choices, or life's myriad decisions, fear often sits in the driver's seat.

Every time I avoided a self-destructive path, felt the temptation to snort myself into oblivion, or triumphed over the sly whisper in my mind tempting me with "just one drink," I turned to writing and sharing as a form of accountability. These moments of victory or struggle

Always speak the *truth*, especially when it's easier to hide behind a lie.

were therapeutic, grounding me in what was true. The road to getting sober taught me about the power of denial, and in my consulting work with clients, I get to witness its potency firsthand.

THE POWER OF DENIAL

Denial is your mind's sneaky way of shielding you from unsettling truths about yourself. It has its roots in your evolutionary need to protect yourself—from shame, guilt, or even just the unknown. It does a brilliant job at ensuring that your worldview remains stable, even if it means ignoring or rejecting information that might challenge it. Denial lets you move forward, bypassing the unpleasant moments, but it comes with a hefty price, and it weighs heavy on every facet of your very being. It lets you portray yourself as better than you are while simultaneously robbing you of seeing your authentic self.

I worked with a dear client who was in denial about past statements he made that were now deemed "problematic" and misogynistic. He struggled to accept that he had made the remarks (despite evidence), especially because those opinions were at odds with his current values. But to make peace with his past, he needed to acknowledge the person he used to be—insensitive, misguided, and careless with his words. To tap into his own Third Perspective, he had to lean into awareness.

Another client's denial looked like downplaying the effects of being publicly shamed online (in a large-scale, well-orchestrated cancellation campaign). She believed that she should just "move on." My job was to help her come to the realization *and acceptance* that she'd been through a traumatic experience and needed to address it with a trauma specialist who could help her achieve post-traumatic growth. Avoidance of responsibility, difficulty apologizing even when it's necessary to do so, and refusing to see the mismatch between your public self and true self—these are all ways denial can manifest.

At the core of my struggle with alcohol was a complex dance with denial. I was often in a state of self-deception, convincing myself I was in control, justifying my actions, and suppressing the inner voices that cried out for a change. My story, in many ways, mirrors the broader struggle we all face with self-sabotage and self-censorship, driven by underlying denial.

Now, you might think, "How is not admitting to an addiction similar to holding back my opinions?" It's about the narratives we tell ourselves. Just as I would convince myself that "one more drink" wouldn't hurt, you might either assure yourself that remaining silent is the "sensible" decision or, on the flip side, be certain that your impulsive words, regardless of their impact, are always justified. The situations differ, yet the core mechanism—that of denial—remains eerily familiar. You might persuade yourself that keeping quiet in a particular situation is the "right" or "safe" choice. While the context is different, the underlying mechanism of denial is strikingly similar:

- **Masking Reality:** Denial prevents us from facing unsettling realities. For me, it was the severe consequences of my alcohol dependence. For you, it might be the emotional weight of consistently muzzling your thoughts or the strain of always needing to be "right."
- **Acts Against Wisdom:** We drift into self-sabotage when we defy our inner wisdom. My deepening relationship with alcohol was a pathway to destruction. Similarly, whenever you suppress your genuine feelings or rashly assert your standpoint without contemplation, you might place a limit on the depth of your interactions.
- **Battling Inner Restraints:** Just as resisting the urge for another drink was my act of rebellion against my old ways, so is your choice to either voice your beliefs, even when daunting, or pause and consider the ramifications of your immediate reactions.

It's important to highlight the similarities of these experiences as it allows you to see the universality of these struggles. Just as I once denied the self-destructive pattern that was unfolding in my life, many of us deny parts of ourselves and our stories. We keep these parts tucked away, hidden behind walls of silence.

It's not always about addiction or dramatic experiences; sometimes, it's about the tiny hesitations, the moments we swallow our words, or the times we talk ourselves out of being seen and heard. Just as I grappled with acknowledging my problematic relationship with alcohol, you might be grappling with when, where, and how to voice your truth. Whether it's in a boardroom, among friends, or in the digital realm, there's a fine line between being unfiltered and being mindful, between suppressing and expressing.

As we go through this book, I'll keep pointing out the difference between choosing when to speak and being *scared* to talk, because being grounded in that distinction is going to make all the difference when it comes to how you communicate.

Now, armed with this understanding, it's time to go deeper. The next chapter is all about exploring your inner thought police. It's where we take a closer look at how your mind may be working for you or against you. The stage for this deep dive has been set by those differences previously mentioned. You'll learn to identify and understand the mechanisms of your internal thought control, which will allow you to regain command over your thoughts and expressions. As you progress, remember to consistently reflect on whether your silence is a conscious choice made with understanding and intent, or a reaction born out of fear.

Chapter 2

Befriend the Mob in Your Mind

In the previous chapter, we explored how and why you might hold back your true feelings. Now, let's dig into what drives this behavior. Imagine finding yourself at a bustling city intersection surrounded by blaring honks, rush-hour traffic, and a sea of people. Among all this, you spot a rowdy mob. They're loud, boisterous, and are creating chaos. But as you inch closer, an unexpected realization hits: this commotion isn't coming from the streets, it's echoing from within you.

Our inner mob is our internal monitoring system—always on alert. This personal squad, made up of doubts, past judgments, biases, and fears, is ever ready to hush our voice or make us rethink our choices. Its influence is so potent that, sometimes, we self-silence even without external pressures.

In relationships, have you ever held back on saying how you truly feel because you're worried about causing a fight or upsetting someone? It's like having a little voice in your head warning you to stay quiet to keep the peace. But when you keep things to yourself, you end up fighting a battle inside. The problems don't go away; they just hide. When I stopped drinking, I quickly learned how much I avoided conflicts. Like many, I was terrified of taking emotional risks and putting myself out there. This fear stopped me from being my true self and kept me feeling stuck. A lot of it came from being afraid of what others might think or say. I'd think, "What if I speak up and it goes wrong?" So I never gave myself the opportunity to see if it could go any other way.

It's these very fears that act like a personal security team in our minds, always on the lookout for danger. But if we want to live freely, we need to befriend these fears, then we can start to face them and handle them better.

BEFRIENDING YOUR INNER MOB

When we encounter parts of ourselves that cause discomfort—our fears, insecurities, or negative thoughts—our instinct is to eliminate or suppress them. It's a natural response. These parts make us feel anxious, and who wants to feel that way? Trying to suppress or ignore these parts rarely works; in fact, it often gives them more power. Going forward, I want you to think of these negative voices like the monsters under your childhood bed. When you ignore them, they seem to grow, their shadows looming larger each night. But when you gather your courage, turn on the lights, and look under the bed, you see that the monstrous shadows were cast by ordinary objects. The anxiety existed in your mind.

Each voice among your inner mob represents a part of you. It might be a part that's afraid of rejection, a part that's worried about being misunderstood, or a part that's wary of conflict. By acknowledging these parts, you can begin to understand their motivations. Why do they advocate for silence over expression? Why do they view disagreement as dangerous? Acknowledging these parts is the first step in befriending them. These voices, as negative as they might seem, arise from a place of protection. They want to shield you from pain, rejection, humiliation. Their methods, though, are like an overprotective parent who keeps their child from climbing trees, fearing they might fall.

You're not dismissing
your fears but choosing
to act *despite* them.

In befriending these parts, you're not giving them free rein. Instead, you're offering them understanding, compassion, and a new perspective. You're telling them, "I hear you; I understand you're scared, but it's okay. We can handle this." You're teaching them that disagreement isn't inherently dangerous, that sharing your perspective isn't a sure path to rejection. You're updating their playbook, so to speak, reminding them that a Third Perspective does exist. As you get to know these parts of yourself, you can start negotiating with them. Instead of letting them impulsively grab the steering wheel, you can discuss and decide your path forward. You're not dismissing your fears but choosing to act *despite* them.

The following exercise will help you to gain insight into your internal voices and understand the beliefs and fears driving them. By regularly engaging with this exercise—emphasis on "regularly"—you will start to identify and challenge the limiting beliefs and fears that are getting in the way. It's another step toward honesty.

A CONVERSATION WITH YOUR INNER MOB

Step 1: Set the Stage
Find a quiet place where you won't be interrupted. Take a few deep breaths and center yourself.

Step 2: Identify a Situation
Think of a recent situation where you held back your true feelings or thoughts. Maybe you didn't share an opinion, didn't express your disagreement with a friend, kept quiet during a work meeting, didn't speak up about something your partner did that bothered you, or didn't set a necessary boundary with a family member.

Step 3: Role-Play

Now, let's have a conversation with the internal voices that influenced that decision:

- Write down the situation at the top of a fresh page. Detail what happened and how you felt.
- Following that, write down what you wanted to say or do but held back from.
- Next, listen to that "mob" in your mind. Without judging whatever comes up, list these voices or specific thoughts. What are they saying? Write down their statements. Examples might include: "They'll laugh at you," "You're overreacting," "It's not that big of a deal," "Don't be so emotional," and so on.

Step 4: Question the Mob

For each statement, ask yourself:

- **Origin:** When have I heard this before? Does this echo someone from my past or a particular experience?
- **Truthfulness:** Is this statement true? How do I know?
- **Protection or Hindrance:** Is this voice trying to protect me from something? If so, what? Or is it holding me back from growth?

Step 5: Reframe and Challenge

Now, try to reframe those statements into something more positive or realistic. For instance, "They'll laugh at you" could be reframed as "Some might not agree, and that's okay. Everyone is entitled to their opinion."

Step 6: Affirmation Creation

Based on your reframed statements, create a set of personal affirmations that you can use to counteract the mob's influence in the future. For example, "I value my opinions and have a right to express them."

Step 7: Reflection

After completing the exercise, take a moment to reflect on the experience. Step back and look at the bigger picture. Did you learn something new about your internal voices? Did you notice any patterns? How do you feel about confronting them on paper?

Step 8: Compassionate Closing

To close this exercise, write a letter of gratitude to your inner mob. Despite their methods, they've been trying to protect you. Acknowledge them, thank them, and then assert that you're learning new, healthier ways to protect and express yourself.

Commitment: For the next week, whenever you find yourself hesitating to speak up or take action, quickly run through this mental exercise. Over time, you'll become more skilled at becoming aware of the voices of your "inner mob" and choosing whether to heed their advice.

This isn't a one-time task. Befriending your inner mob is a continuous process, a dialogue that evolves as you do. There will be setbacks, days when the mob seems particularly loud. That's okay. It's all part of it. On those days, take a step back, breathe, and remind yourself that it's okay to feel scared. It's okay to have doubts. And then, remind yourself that it's also okay to express yourself, to share your thoughts and perspectives bravely.

After that exercise, you've probably noticed some patterns. Those voices in your head? They don't just influence your immediate reactions, but they also help shape what you believe deep down.

WHERE BELIEFS AND OPINIONS MEET

Knowing the difference between beliefs, opinions, and values is key because they're a big part of how you see the world and your place in it. Think of beliefs as the basic ideas you have about how the world works. They're like the foundation of a house—built in your early years and influenced by things like how you were raised, your culture, and your own experiences. Opinions are what you build on top of this foundation. They're your personal takes or judgments based on your beliefs. Values, which we will cover in more depth in Part 2, are a bit different. They're like the rules or guidelines we live by. Imagine values as the blueprint for the house—they help decide how everything is laid out and the function. Right now, we're focusing on your beliefs and opinions, and how your inner mob affects them. This mob is a mix of all sorts of things—memories, what your family taught you, what society tells you—all coming together like pieces of a jigsaw puzzle to form your view of the world.

Take, for instance, someone growing up in a traditional, conservative household. This environment is the foundation for this person's belief system. For them, the "rules" from home might feel like the only way to see things. Over time, these beliefs become so deeply ingrained that they are accepted as absolute truths. But then, life happens. As this person steps out of their immediate family environment and experiences the world, they are exposed to different perspectives. They meet new friends, read new books, and have new, more progressive experiences. Suddenly, those "home rules" might not be the only way to see the picture.

You grow up with certain ideas, thinking they're the "right" ones. But as you meet new people, learn new things, and have new experiences, your views start to shift. Sometimes, this change can make you feel torn. You can experience an internal conflict between beliefs that you identified with and that have, in part, shaped your identity and your own views. On the one hand, you don't want to upset your family or friends (or whoever else!) who think like you used to. So, when you're with them, you might nod and agree. But then when you're on your own, or with a different group, you might let your new views shine.

Living like this can feel like wearing two different hats. It's tiring, confusing, and sometimes makes you wonder: "Who am I, really?" But, here's the cool part: this tug-of-war inside is a sign that you're growing. It's a chance to really think about what YOU believe, not just what you've been told. It's a chance to reevaluate and update your belief system.

Now, beliefs and opinions are like siblings. Beliefs are the older, more set-in-their-ways one. They're deep inside us and don't change easily. Opinions are the younger, more adaptable sibling. They're our beliefs in action, the stuff we share with others, and they can change as we learn and experience more. The personal convictions you are willing to declare and defend in public can also give you a peek into the makeup of your belief system—we'll dive into how this plays out, especially when we get to the Responsibility pillar (Part 2). It will be a crucial part of our work together. Understanding this connection and difference between our opinions and beliefs is key in bridging the gap between our public personas and our private realities.

A similar story unfolds in workplaces or social circles with an overbearing cultural or political leaning. Imagine a scenario in a workplace where the majority are enthusiastically supporting a new diversity initiative. While the intention seems positive, you notice some practical flaws in the approach, such as tokenism or a lack of genuine inclusivity. However, speaking up against it feels like navigating a minefield. You know that challenging this initiative could label you as "unsupportive" or "against diversity," even when your concerns are about the execution, not the concept itself. It's like walking on a tightrope—voice your concerns and risk backlash, or stay silent and feel complicit in what you see as a superficial solution. It's tempting to nod along, especially when that inner mob convinces you that voicing your support (even if it's fake) will help you fit in better; who knows, it might even lead to a promotion. Behind closed doors, you share your real thoughts only with people you trust. These silent compromises might appear as sensible survival strategies, ways to navigate tricky social, professional, or political landscapes. But doing this over and over can make us feel trapped, like we're wearing a mask. At our core as humans, we have a survival instinct that prioritizes harmony and acceptance over the potential to be shunned by the group. We learn to adapt, sometimes to the extent of forcing ourselves to believe in ideas that we know aren't our truth. We accommodate the uncomfortable until it becomes our new normal.

Now, it's time to truly explore this dynamic in yourself. To peel back the layers and understand your own responses in such situations, you'll need to turn inward. Have you ever stopped to think about why you might nod along to that popular idea, even if it clashes with what you truly believe? It's essential to differentiate between your core beliefs and the opinions you share, especially in pressured environments, and the following exercise will help you to discern the nuances between your core beliefs and the opinions you hold, understanding how each influences the other and your outward behavior. This analysis is going to encourage introspection and critical thinking, and will require a bit of writing, so put the time aside and you'll be rewarded highly!

BELIEFS VERSUS OPINIONS INVENTORY

Find a quiet space and engage your open and introspective mind. This exercise should take 30–45 minutes.

Step 1: Warm-Up
- Start with a few minutes of relaxation. Close your eyes, take deep breaths, and clear your mind. Center yourself in the present.

Step 2: Brainstorming Session

- Open your eyes and, at the top of your page, write "Opinions I've voiced recently."
- Following this, list out five to ten statements or thoughts you've expressed in the past week or two. These can range from casual comments on the weather, food preferences, or reactions to a news article, to more complex topics like political or cultural viewpoints.

Step 3: Digging Deeper

- Now, create a new section titled "Why I think this way."
- Revisit each opinion and write a few sentences explaining why you hold this view. Try to remember what influenced this opinion. Was it something you read, an experience, or perhaps something someone said to you?

Step 4: Unearthing Beliefs

- Start a fresh section called "Underlying beliefs."
- Analyze the reasons behind each opinion. Try to identify if there's a deeper belief fueling this opinion. Ask yourself: "What fundamental belief of mine aligns with this opinion?" Write down the core beliefs that come to light.

Step 5: Reflection and Comparison

- Finally, title a new section "Beliefs versus opinions."
- Review your underlying beliefs alongside your opinions. Reflect on the following:
  o Are there any opinions that directly contradict your deeper beliefs?
  o Do your opinions shift more than your beliefs?
  o Can you identify opinions that have changed recently, while the underlying belief remained the same?

Step 6: Concluding Thoughts

- End with a reflective piece. Consider how this exercise made you feel and whether it helped you see your beliefs and opinions in a new light. Were there any surprises? Any moments of clarity?

Keep this exercise in mind as you encounter various opinions in your daily life, whether your own or others'. Ask yourself: "What belief might be driving this opinion?" This ongoing practice can help solidify your understanding of the beliefs–opinions dynamic.

Remember when we talked about those silent compromises we make, and the internal battles between what we really feel versus what we show to the world? Now, let's think about a sneaky little thing that sometimes powers those silent nods and avoids conversations: our inner mob's notorious friend, intolerance.

THE IRONY OF INTOLERANCE

Intolerance often sneaks into our daily conversations and personal relationships. It's like a silent critic, whispering that if someone sees things differently, they're probably wrong. It's the quiet nudge to steer clear of topics or people that make us feel uneasy. And here's the twist: While it's a breeze to spot intolerance in others, catching it in ourselves? Not so much. When faced with differing opinions or unfamiliar situations, the inner mob can quickly rally its forces, pushing you to reject, dismiss, or even mock what's different. Instead of trying to understand, it promotes snap judgments. It convinces you that there's safety in sticking to what's familiar, to what you know.

Intolerance and the inner mob are like partners in crime. They feed off each other. The inner mob, with its hasty reactions, can fuel intolerance, making it harder for you to appreciate or even acknowledge other perspectives. In turn, unchecked intolerance gives the inner mob more power, letting it grow louder and more dominant.

It's easy to label others as intolerant. There will be some people who saw the subtitle of this book and immediately thought of a person or group that fits into the "age of intolerance." Did you think of yourself? Probably not. But how open are we *really* to ideas and opinions that initially unsettle us? Have you ever felt an instant "nope" when hearing an unfamiliar point of view? I have, as recently as last night! Or maybe you've side-stepped a discussion that felt a tad too unfamiliar? These could be little signs of your own hidden biases or moments of unintentional intolerance.

This is not about shaming yourself or doubling down if you recognize your own narrow-mindedness. It's about accepting that your way of seeing the world is not the only way, and that your truths may not be universal truths. Wild thought, I know. I always chuckle to myself when I think back to my own moments of self-righteousness. I find humor to be a useful tool in removing the shame and charge from behaviors I've outgrown. When you let go of the incessant need to cling on to a single story, you open doors to more interesting conversations, deeper understanding, and greater empathy. It makes life much more colorful and fun. We become better listeners, better learners, and better communicators.

Understanding the difference between tolerance and just going along with things is super important though. Tolerance isn't just a nod of agreement to all views; it's about making room for different voices to enter the conversation, without doing away with your boundaries. It's about championing justice and truth, all while nurturing connection and mutual respect.

Meet Jonah, a high school teacher from a small town in California. A few years back, he dropped me a heartfelt email appreciating my work, which led him to join one of my mentorship groups. Jonah's

When you let go of the
incessant need to cling
on to a single story, you
open doors to more
interesting conversations,
deeper understanding,
and greater empathy.

been teaching biology for a decade now, and his dedication to his profession has earned him the respect of his students, colleagues, and me. As his school began to diversify, with students from different cultural, religious, and social backgrounds joining the community, he found himself facing a challenge he had not anticipated.

One afternoon, after a biology class, a group of students approached him. They explained their discomfort with certain aspects of the curriculum, specifically the parts about human evolution. Their religious beliefs, they said, conflicted with these teachings. Jonah, having never faced such a scenario before, initially dismissed their concerns. He insisted that science was a matter of facts, not beliefs, and that the curriculum couldn't be altered to accommodate personal viewpoints.

Jonah's dismissal led to a rift. Word spread quickly, and the school community became divided. Some supported him, stating that religious beliefs should not interfere with education. Others sided with the students, arguing for a more inclusive approach to teaching. As the tension escalated, he found himself reflecting on his reactions. He realized he had dismissed the students' concerns without trying to understand their perspective. He had let his biases and preconceptions dictate his response. His intolerance had furthered division instead of fostering dialogue.

Motivated to make amends, he decided to approach the situation differently. He invited the students for a discussion, listened to their concerns, and expressed his willingness to understand their perspective. He acknowledged the conflict they were facing and reassured them that their beliefs were not being dismissed. He didn't change the curriculum—it was a science class, after all. But he did adapt his teaching approach. He started framing his lessons in a way that emphasized the scientific method—hypothesizing, observing, testing— rather than presenting the theories as unchallengeable truths. He created a safe space for dialogue and questions, allowing for a more inclusive learning environment.

Jonah's journey was testament to the transformation that can occur when we acknowledge our intolerance and strive toward understanding. He realized that intolerance didn't always appear in the form of egregious acts; it could be subtle, like unwillingness to engage with a different viewpoint. By choosing to listen and understand, he not only resolved the conflict but also enriched his teaching methods, thereby benefiting the entire school community. The ripple effects of his actions were far-reaching. Other teachers began to adopt a more inclusive approach, students felt more seen and understood, and the school community became more cohesive.

This story is more than an account of one person's struggle with intolerance. It reflects a larger societal issue, and one that each of us may grapple with in our own lives. Like Jonah, we all have areas in our lives where we are used to having control, where our values and beliefs go unchallenged. But what happens when someone or something comes in and shakes up your well-established world? Your initial reaction might be one of fear, anger, or intolerance. This is a natural human response. But the danger comes when we choose to double down on our narrow-mindedness, dismissing the new or different outright instead of pausing to consider its merits.

REFLECTIVE QUESTIONS

- Are there areas in your life where you're resisting change or diversity of thought?
- Is there someone in your life who challenges your status quo and makes you uncomfortable?
- Are you meeting this discomfort with curiosity, or are you doubling down on your initial views?

The path toward tolerance is not an easy one. It requires constant self-reflection, unlearning entrenched biases and engaging in challenging conversations. Even though I have been doing this work for nearly a decade, I, too, understand that this will be a lifelong practice of introspection and course-correcting. It's not a one-and-done. And I find that exciting. There's no certificate that says "I've arrived!" and there's not supposed to be. In a world rife with intolerance, each one of us has a responsibility—a responsibility to challenge our biases and to stand up for mental flexibility.

It begins with us, in our everyday interactions, in our words and our actions. As we cultivate tolerance within ourselves, we inspire others to do the same, creating a domino effect that can transform our world. It isn't about being passive or accepting everything brought to our doorstep. It's about actively choosing to be curious, to listen, and to engage respectfully. It's about choosing understanding over division, dialogue over dismissal.

When we talk about The Third Perspective, we're talking about seeing more than two sides to a story. It's about realizing that most things aren't black or white, but a mix of both. There's a lot that lies in between, full of details and subtleties that can deepen our understanding. Today, we often get caught in an "either–or" mindset. This makes it hard to see the bigger picture. Think back to the insights you collected earlier about your inner mob—that voice that often protects you in unhelpful ways. It's influenced by what you've been taught, what you've experienced, and what you truly believe. By understanding this voice, you can tell the difference between a passing opinion and a deep-rooted belief. And knowing this difference is key. It helps you decide when to stand firm and when there's a chance to learn and grow.

Jonah's story is a great example. He faced a choice: stay stuck in his viewpoint or tune into his Third Perspective and consider a wider range of experiences. Choosing to be open-minded didn't mean giving up on what he believed. It simply added more depth to his understanding.

In the next chapter, we're going to tackle something that can't be ignored in today's societal landscape: the phenomenon of cancel culture. Yes, it's the elephant in the room, often contentious and misunderstood. But I'm willing to go there with you because this is a layer of reality that adds to your overall progress. By diving into this topic, you'll have more clarity on how this culture impacts your willingness to speak up and the risks associated with it.

This conversation is not about taking sides, but about expanding your worldview. You'll recognize the fine line between accountability and the unforgiving rush to judgment. As you step into this discussion, keep an open mind and be prepared to challenge your assumptions.

Chapter 3

No One Left to Cancel

R emember those times when you've wanted to share an opinion or thought about something significant happening around you, but you hesitated? Maybe you felt you didn't know enough or you were worried that you might get things wrong. Perhaps you felt the weight of the demand to have an opinion—NOW, to repost an infographic, to share a fundraising link, to pick a side so that people know that you are a "safe" person. You're not alone in this. I can raise my hand and say that there were times when I'd feel immense pressure to quickly take a strong stance. Times when I would routinely wonder why certain people were not making their position known, why they were not "using their platform" to speak up. I would find myself feeling entitled to assume I knew other people's opinions, believing that if they were silent on something I thought was important, that silence was a stance in itself. If you want to understand your relationship with self-censorship, or perhaps to refine your current social filter, you need to acknowledge and understand the context in which you're communicating.

Today, we do not have a shortage of loaded topics vying for our attention. I'm talking about issues that touch our lives, our communities, and our planet in profound ways. Think about it: We're dealing with climate change, which is making our summers hotter and storms fiercer. Or the ever-evolving discourse on gender and sexuality (particularly the rise in trans and nonbinary identities), challenging long-held norms and inviting new understandings. Think about the mental well-being debates amplified by social media (questions like "Have we gone too far with therapy-speak?" are being asked), or the privacy concerns in our tech-driven lives, or the economic divides that the COVID-19 pandemic has further exposed. And let's not forget the shifting perceptions on substances like cannabis, where legality and morality often intersect. *Then* there's feminism, which continues to evolve and spark discussions on equality and representation. The political landscape, too, especially in recent years, has become a hotbed of divisive topics, forcing us to confront our beliefs and biases. And, of course, religion, which for many remains a deeply personal yet publicly debated topic. Gosh, I even tired myself out writing all of that. Each topic feels like a minefield, where one misstep can lead to unintended explosions. When these big topics are fighting for your attention at the same time, it can feel like your single voice might get lost in the noise. But not only that—if you do decide to say something, there's usually a big worry that you will be dragged through the streets of social media by your collar if you get it wrong. This overwhelming feeling? It's a big reason many of us end up pressing the mute button on our opinions.

This is where I begin to worry. Why are we expecting people to be born educated on these topics? Why are we anticipating perfection, demanding the use of language that doesn't offend anyone and upholding an ideal of political correctness? The reality of being human is that we are inherently imperfect. I would even go as far as to say that every single one of us is politically *incorrect* by nature. Our nature includes the vulnerability of making mistakes, the grace of growth, and the journey of learning. When I reflect on my own life, it's a lovely jumble of rights and wrongs, of triumphs and tribulations, and of lessons learned both gently and harshly. Every mistake, every misstep, was an opportunity for me to grow, to realign, and to progress. And isn't that what being human is all about?

Every single one
of us is politically
incorrect by nature.

EMBRACING IMPERFECTIONS

I've come to learn that, as human beings, we are not supposed to be processing the amount of information we take in today thanks to the advancement of technology. We aren't meant to wake up first thing in the morning knowing in frightening detail what is happening on the other side of the world. We aren't supposed to be exposed to stories that morph and change rapidly, often stripped of all nuance and context.

Consider your childhood—that period of blissful ignorance, innocent questions, and boundless curiosity. We stumbled, fumbled words, asked the "wrong" questions, and might have even held views that our mature selves would now cringe at. But that's the thing—we were allowed the space to evolve, to outgrow our limited perspectives, to absorb, and to adapt. It's this very grace that seems to be diminishing in our current discourse, and I can't help but wonder, why?

It's essential to remember that the information age has compressed the world into a digital village. With just a tap, we're exposed to infinite perspectives, experiences, and information. This exposure, while enlightening, can be overwhelming. Our primitive brains are trying to grasp, internalize, and form opinions on subjects that span various cultural, historical, and political boundaries. It's a lot! One moment you're reading about polar bears and melting ice caps, and the next, you're trying to wrap your head around why certain hashtags are trending. It's like trying to drink from a firehose. Now, combine that with the innate human desire to belong, to be accepted, and to avoid conflict (explored in Chapter 1). The result? An environment where the fear of saying the "wrong thing" trumps the genuine desire to understand and connect.

Yet, it's in these imperfect moments, where we might get it "wrong," that we have the most significant opportunities for connection—with ourselves and with the world around us. When we step back and observe our reactions—our defensiveness, our intolerance, our guilt, or our avoidance—it tells us so much about our inner world. And when we can witness someone else's mistake with empathy and an open heart, it speaks volumes about the expansiveness of our spirit.

It's true, we must strive for understanding and sensitivity, but we must also extend grace—to ourselves and others. We won't always have the right words, the complete knowledge, or the perfect stance. What we can offer, however, is a listening ear, a humble heart ready to learn, and the vulnerability to admit when we're wrong.

In a world bursting with discussions, many of us are choosing to hold back, hesitant to voice our thoughts. This observation has fueled my determination to show you that silence isn't the only path. If you truly want a world that thrives on conversations that stretch you, allow for deep understanding, and bring you fulfilling connections, it has to be a world where our shared human imperfections are acknowledged. It has to be a world where we don't cancel everyone who steps out of the invisible lines. Creating a space where it's safe to be wrong, without facing undue retribution, is essential (you'll get a detailed outline of how to do this when you get to Part 3: Expression). We need to create a culture where differing opinions can coexist, where constructive criticism leads to growth, and where expressing oneself doesn't have to mean walking a tightrope over a sea of judgment.

Maybe, just maybe, as we progress, we'll find a way to navigate these conversations more confidently, yet cautiously, without defaulting to holding our tongues or speaking prematurely without considering the impact. As you know by now, this is not me saying that you need to be vocal about everything that touches your mind and heart. You don't. I'm saying that every perspective adds a unique shade to societal discussion, including perspectives we disagree with or simply don't like. Yes, these topics are enormous, but every big issue is made up of individual stories, experiences, and opinions—including yours.

As we move through the book together, I will give you a gentle nudge to remind you that it's okay to step forward, to share, and to be part of these crucial dialogues. You'll begin to choose your battles wisely, to remember that you do not have to die on every hill you come across, even if people are demanding that you make the trek. We'll look at ways to build your confidence, educate yourself without feeling overwhelmed, and, most importantly, communicate with both empathy and assertiveness.

Up next is an exercise with a series of reflection prompts tailored to different scenarios, each carefully crafted to continue looking your own biases and hesitations in the eye. It's time to get to the bottom of why you self-censor, especially when faced with big, challenging topics. Why have you erected those internal barriers?

WHAT IS HOLDING YOU BACK?

Find a space where you can think, and give yourself the grace to explore your inner thoughts. Remember: this is your personal space for raw, unfiltered self-reflection. Don't write as if someone else will read it. Gently wade into your internal world to discover what might be quietly influencing your silence.

Too Big to Grasp
- **Overview:** The enormity of issues and why they feel daunting.
- **Reflection Question:** Think about a time when you felt overwhelmed by the scope of a global issue. What held you back from discussing or exploring it further?

Fear of Getting It Wrong
- **Overview:** The pitfalls of misinformation in a digital age.
- **Reflection Question:** Recall an instance when you hesitated to speak because you were unsure or afraid of being incorrect. How did that make you feel?

Echo Chambers

- **Overview:** The dangers of only being presented with information from familiar voices that mirror your worldview and don't challenge your thinking.
- **Reflection Question:** Have you ever discovered you were in an "echo chamber"? How did it influence your perspective or willingness to share?

Desire for Harmony

- **Overview:** The natural inclination to maintain peace and avoid confrontation.
- **Reflection Question:** What topics do you usually avoid discussing to keep the peace, and with whom?

Imposter Syndrome

- **Overview:** The feeling of inadequacy despite being competent.
- **Reflection Question:** Have you ever felt like you weren't "qualified" enough to share your opinion? Why?

Overwhelm and Burnout

- **Overview:** The fatigue from constant information bombardment.
- **Reflection Question:** How do you usually cope when feeling overwhelmed by news or social issues?

Now I'm going to play fair by showing the other side of this challenge. In those moments of high stakes and emotions, some people find their voices rising, their ears closing, and their social filters dissolving—the restraint collapses and communication becomes a one-way street. For those of you who recognize yourself in this description, know that your passionate voice is vital, but so is a listening ear and a considered response.

UNDERSTANDING YOUR QUICK REACTIONS AND THEIR EFFECTS

Remember, the goal of these questions is to encourage self-awareness and reflection. Once again, find a quiet space.

Reactionary Responses
- **Overview:** Quick-fire comments that can skew our understanding of pressing issues.
- **Reflection Question:** Can you think of a recent conversation where you reacted immediately without pausing?

Anger-Led Dialogue
- **Overview:** When passion eclipses purpose in important conversations.
- **Reflection Question:** Can you recall a conversation where your anger overshadowed the objective?

Dismissal of Opposing Voices
- **Overview:** Shutting out differing opinions, especially during heated debates.
- **Reflection Question:** When was the last time you dismissed someone's perspective without genuinely listening?

Oversimplification
- **Overview:** Reducing intricate topics to one-liners and risking misunderstanding.
- **Reflection Question:** Can you think about a time when you simplified a topic for the sake of argument?

Assumption of Expertise
- **Overview:** Diving into deep waters with just a little bit of knowledge.

- **Reflection Question:** Can you reflect on a moment when you felt you knew enough about a subject to lead a conversation, only to learn that you didn't know as much as you thought?

Abandonment of Empathy
- **Overview:** Forgetting the human touch when addressing sensitive subjects.
- **Reflection Question:** Have you ever shared your perspective or knowledge about a sensitive topic and later realized it might've been insensitive?

Ignoring Emotional State
- **Overview:** Carrying emotional baggage from one topic to the next.
- **Reflection Question:** Can you think of a time when you let your emotions from one discussion spill into another?

COLLECTIVE SABOTAGE

You may have heard the term "cancel culture" frequently used in conversations, debates, and media headlines. But today, I introduce you to a term I've coined: "collective sabotage." Why the need for a new term, you ask? Because I genuinely believe we're all getting a bit confused about what "cancel culture" really means. To one person, it simply means holding individuals accountable for their actions. Yet, to another, it means unfairly ruining reputations, without giving chances for mistakes to be mended.

After giving it some serious thought and turning to my professional work as inspiration, I landed on the term "collective sabotage" as a more accurate descriptor. I think it gets to the heart of the issue. It's about the times when we, as a society, might be accidentally working against our best interests. This can be through actions, behaviors, or systems that, though perhaps seen as beneficial in the short term, might hurt us in the long run. While "cancel culture" has been a snappy phrase, it gets a lot of mixed reactions and often its meaning is skewed by personal experiences or political leanings. By introducing "collective sabotage," I hope to give us a clearer way to talk about this whole situation.

So, here's the tough question: When does holding people accountable slip into something that actually hurts us all? It's not always clear. Yes, making sure people take responsibility for what they say and do is super important. But when does it become overkill? When does that shift into an approach where our excitement to see justice served ends up damaging our shared values of understanding, second chances, and collective growth?

ENTER GROUPTHINK

Jasmine, one of my clients, recently shared a story from her workplace that perfectly encapsulates the notion of "collective sabotage" driven by another term we need to familiarize ourselves with: groupthink.

Jasmine worked for a midsize tech company that had always prided itself on its innovative ideas. One day, her team leader, Alex, proposed a new project. On the surface, it seemed like a fresh and groundbreaking idea: a new app that would integrate all of a user's social media feeds into one platform. The initial reactions were overwhelmingly positive. "It's the future!" one colleague exclaimed. "We'll revolutionize the way people use social media!" another chimed in.

Jasmine had reservations. After I asked a few clarifying questions, she told me that she'd felt the app might compromise user privacy, and also noted that similar platforms had failed in the past. But as she looked around the room, seeing the nods of agreement and the excitement in her colleagues' eyes, she hesitated to voice her concerns. No one wanted to be the naysayer, the one who rained on the parade. Instead of speaking up, she decided to stay silent. She thought, "Maybe

I'm just being overly cautious. Everyone else seems to believe in this. Who am I to push back on something so big?"

Months of time and resources were poured into the project. The enthusiasm in the office was palpable. Yet, when the app was finally launched, it was met with severe backlash over privacy concerns. Users were uncomfortable with a single platform having access to all their social media information. The app was also unstable due to trying to integrate too many different platforms. Ultimately, it was discontinued, and the company faced both financial and reputational damage.

At its core, groupthink is when the desire for conformity in a group results in making a decision that eventually causes chaos. It's when everyone starts thinking the same way, not because they necessarily agree, but because they feel they *should* agree. The fear of rocking the boat, standing out, or challenging the status quo leads to decisions that aren't always in the group's best interest.

On reflection, Jasmine realized that what had happened was a classic case of collective sabotage. The entire team, in their shared enthusiasm and reluctance to voice dissent, had fallen into the trap of groupthink. They had collectively moved forward with an idea without critically assessing its potential pitfalls. As a result, they had been given a hefty lesson in the perils of silent consensus.

Following the failure of the app, and after several sessions with me, Jasmine and a few colleagues had an honest discussion about what went wrong. Many admitted they had had their reservations but had suppressed them due to the wave of optimism that swept through the team. Thinking back to my corporate days, I'm reminded of how common this was: when everyone in a group starts moving in the same direction without questioning, it can lead to blind spots. And a big price to pay.

To their credit, the company took the setback as an opportunity to reassess their decision-making processes. They recognized the importance of multiple viewpoints and began encouraging open dialogue and constructive feedback in team meetings. They realized that disagreement, when approached *constructively*, isn't detrimental but rather a valuable tool to refine ideas.

In the bigger picture, Jasmine's story is just a drop in the bucket of what can happen in society at large. When we get so caught up in a prevailing sentiment or popular belief without critically examining it, we risk making decisions that aren't in our collective best interest. When we silence our concerns or our unique viewpoints because "everyone else seems to be on board," we might just be sabotaging ourselves collectively.

Let's take a closer look at an example from recent history to understand the impact of collective groupthink and its consequences. Think back to the early 2000s, specifically the invasion of Iraq in 2003. At that time, there was a widespread wave of support for the invasion. This sentiment was driven by a combination of patriotism, fear, and a flow of misinformation that convinced many people it was the right thing to do. Despite this, there were individuals who had doubts, but their voices were drowned out by the overwhelming majority. As time passed and the long-term, tragic consequences of the invasion unfolded, the voices of dissent began to emerge more clearly.

This situation highlights a crucial lesson about the dangers of collective groupthink. When we're surrounded by a powerful, dominant narrative, it can be easy to go along with it, especially if everyone else seems to be in agreement. However, when we don't voice our concerns or different viewpoints because we believe that everyone else is on the same page, we risk making decisions that might not be in our best interest as a society. This example serves as a reminder of the importance of questioning and critically examining the prevailing sentiments, even when they are popular, to avoid collective mistakes on a grand scale.

Disagreement, when approached *constructively*, isn't detrimental but rather a valuable tool to refine ideas.

I'm curious to know what you would have done if you were in Jasmine's shoes. You're surrounded by an overwhelming wave of consensus and, yet, a nagging feeling tells you to reconsider. In life, we often find ourselves swept up in the wave of group dynamics, perhaps without even realizing it. As an adult, I now see that I spent most of my early life wildly underestimating the power and influence of "the group," be it on the playground or in the boardroom. It's easy to flow with the current, especially when the waters are calm. But every so often, you might feel a subtle undercurrent pulling you in a different direction.

I'd like to introduce you to another exercise: Role Reversal. I designed this to help you step outside of your comfort zone and view situations from a different vantage point. By doing so, you'll gain a clearer perspective on your own feelings and decisions, separate from the group's influence.

Shall we?

ROLE REVERSAL

Think of a time when you didn't voice an opinion because it didn't align with everyone else's. Now, imagine you were in a role where it was your *job* to challenge ideas (e.g., a consultant brought in to find potential flaws).

- Would you have acted differently?
- What would you have said?
- How might the outcome have changed if you had voiced your opinion from this perspective?

Did you notice anything interesting about the answers you got from the aforementioned exercise? I've spoken with many who have tried this exercise, and I often find it both surprising and revealing how a mere title change, like from "employee" to "consultant," can shift our entire perspective. Suddenly, you might feel more empowered, more "allowed" to share that gut feeling. Isn't it curious how a label, or our perceived role, can influence not just our actions, but also our confidence in our own beliefs?

It makes me wonder: How often do we silence ourselves, not because we don't trust our insights, but because of how we believe others will perceive us? Because of the seat or role we occupy in a particular setting? Because of our identity (which is something we'll explore in Chapter 5)?

Reflect back on times where you might have stopped yourself from saying something, not necessarily because you doubted its merit, but perhaps because of your perceived "place" in the group. Was it a family gathering? A meeting at work? An online discussion? Such self-awareness is golden. The more you spot these moments, the better equipped you are to question your hesitations and allow your authentic voice to shine through, regardless of your title or position.

THE "FIVE WHYS"

This is a bonus reflective exercise before the chapter comes to a close. Think about a decision where you felt swept along by groupthink. Ask yourself, "Why did I agree with this decision?" Write down your answer. Now, ask "why" to that answer, and then continue asking "why" to each subsequent answer, until you've asked "why" five times. The goal here is to uncover underlying reasons or fears that led to your agreement.

For example, imagine you're part of a team at work and there's a proposal to implement a new, but complex, project-management tool. Everyone seems excited about it, except you have reservations about its complexity and the learning curve involved. However, you end up agreeing to it without voicing your concerns.

Step 1: Why did I agree with this decision?

Answer: Because everyone else on the team seemed enthusiastic about it.

Step 2: Why did their enthusiasm influence my decision?

Answer: I didn't want to be the only one opposing the idea and risk alienating myself from the team.

Step 3: Why was I worried about alienating myself?

Answer: I value being a part of the team and worry that disagreeing might make me seem uncooperative or difficult.

Step 4: Why do I think disagreeing would make me seem uncooperative?

Answer: In the past, when I've disagreed with group decisions, it led to conflicts and strained relationships.

Step 5: Why did those past experiences affect my current decision-making?

Answer: Those experiences made me cautious about expressing dissenting opinions, because I fear conflict and its impact on my work relationships.

This example shows you how the "five whys" can help trace back the root of your decision to agree with the group. It reveals deeper fears and motivations like the desire to maintain harmony and avoid conflict. Once you see these underlying factors in all their glory, you can address them and make more conscious decisions in the future. Try this exercise for any other decision blocks you have!

Speaking up, even if it goes against the grain, could be the very thing that prevents us from collective pitfalls. You should remember that it's not about being contrary for the sake of it, but about making sure that decisions, whether in the workplace or broader society, are well-rounded and consider all angles. To avoid collective sabotage— I'll go ahead and assume you want to—you must recognize the *signs*, which we'll cover in more detail in the next chapter. These behaviors are particularly strong in virtual spaces, where the echo chambers of social media and online forums amp up groupthink and people end up mirroring each other's thoughts. This creates a sort of bubble where everyone seems to agree, and different opinions don't get much attention. This rush to agree with the majority, without really thinking things through, can lead us to decisions that aren't in our collective best interest.

In the penultimate chapter of our Awareness pillar, we're going to take a closer look at how groupthink and mob mentality show up online. You'll learn about how it works and how to spot it. This knowledge will help you think more independently in virtual environments so you can contribute to conversations in a way that's more thoughtful, balanced, and informed.

Chapter 4

You Owe the Internet Nothing

Remember the iconic scenes from old movies? A "mob" would be portrayed as a frenzied group of villagers, torches and pitchforks in hand, rallying together under the dim torchlight. A particular episode of *The Simpsons* might even pop into your mind. Their collective energy, fear, and anger is palpable, and they are often driven by a single-minded purpose—be it chasing some mythical creature or seeking justice in their own, often misguided, way. These scenes remind me of the powerful, and sometimes reckless, outcomes when a group of people get carried away in the moment.

Jump to the present day. Torches and pitchforks might be a thing of the past, but that mob spirit? Oh, it's alive and well. Instead of gathering in the town square, people rally online. Thanks to social media, a place that doesn't seem to consider nuance, your opinion can quickly be backed by thousands, or even millions, of others, making it loud and very hard to ignore. Within hours, or even minutes, online platforms can be flooded with the collective sentiments of anger, support, indignation, or joy. And much like those movie mobs, online crowds can let raw emotion cloud their better judgment.

Every time period, including ours, faces its own unique challenges and movements. We're living in a time when social media makes everything louder. It broadcasts our voices, our mistakes, and our disagreements for all to see. This is completely new to the human species. And that's powerful—it can change stories, challenge the way things are, and, sometimes, sadly, it can tear things down.

I'd be doing you a disservice if I didn't address this mob mentality, evident in every nook and cranny of the web. "Mob mentality" (often referred to as herd or pack mentality) is when groups of people can sometimes act collectively in overly emotional, impulsive, or even aggressive ways. This phenomenon happens because a person is influenced by their peers to adopt certain behaviors—even behaviors they wouldn't usually engage in. It's driven by the desire to conform and it's a key part of the collective sabotage we spoke about in the previous chapter. Sometimes a person will go to the extent of overriding personal beliefs or common sense. From gossip blogs to online forums, and even knitting circles, the patterns are eerily similar.

MOB MENTALITY: ONLINE AND OFFLINE

Online Mob Mentality

- **Amplification Through Anonymity:** Online, people often feel more anonymous, which can lead to a lack of accountability. This anonymity emboldens people to join in on collective behaviors that they might not engage in offline.
- **Rapid Spread:** Information (or misinformation) spreads quickly on the internet, fueling mob mentality. Social media platforms can amplify emotional reactions, leading to rapid formation of online mobs.
- **Echo Chambers:** You'll see this one show up more than once in this book. Online spaces often become echo chambers where only similar viewpoints are reinforced, and opposing views are rarely encountered or openly welcomed. This can intensify group beliefs, leading to extreme positions.
- **Dehumanization:** There's a tendency to forget that there's a

real person behind each profile. This can lead to harsher interactions than someone might have face-to-face.

Offline Mob Mentality

- **Group Pressure:** In physical settings, people may conform to the behaviors and opinions of a group to fit in or avoid conflict. This is often seen in social, professional, or political gatherings. This is also common among younger people, where the pressure to conform to friends' or peers' behaviors can be very strong.
- **Loss of Individuality:** In a group, people can lose their sense of individuality and moral judgment. Instead, they will adopt the group's identity and decisions. This then leads to actions that, as individuals, they might find unacceptable.
- **Riots and Protests:** Mob mentality can manifest in intense situations like protests or riots, where the collective emotion and energy of the crowd can lead to actions that individuals might not typically engage in.

Now, let me set things straight: this isn't an internet-bashing session. I rely on social media daily. Heck, if not for its vast reach, you probably wouldn't be reading my words right now. As much as it has its pitfalls, it's just as important to recognize and utilize its positive aspects: the connectivity and ability to create global communities with shared interests and experiences (exactly what I was able to do); the amplifying of voices that have historically been marginalized or unheard; enabling small businesses to reach more people; the real-time updates in times of crisis, which can give you information faster than traditional media; and, of course, the wealth of creative inspiration that can be easily showcased and celebrated—with little to no gatekeeping.

But it's clear that emotions, especially *fiery* ones like outrage and resentment, have a powerful *hook*. They really draw us in online. They are the fuel that keeps the internet's gears churning away. These emotions drive engagement, a strategy used masterfully by many platforms. Their algorithms prioritize content that sparks strong emotional reactions—and more time online means more ads, and more money for them. Think about this the next time you find yourself stuck in endless scrolling or arguing with a raging stranger in the comment section. It's not by chance, it's by design. This engagement is further boosted by features like dopamine-triggering interactions (likes, shares, comments), infinite scrolling that offers endless content, personalized feeds that show you exactly what you like, and constant notifications pulling you back in. Unfortunately, those raw emotions like anger and disgust often outshine more constructive qualities like empathy and understanding. Simply put, anger packs a punch—and that punch lines pockets.

Today, almost everyone interacts with online platforms. Even my eighty-four-year-old grandma back in Zimbabwe checks in on her Facebook account. There was once a clear separation between our online and offline selves, but gone are the days when we logged out at the end of each day. Now, even if you're not constantly on social media, you're still expected to be up-to-date with everything happening online, from the latest scandals to news stories, movements, and trending hashtags. Everyone seems to anticipate that you're caught up with the latest. And sometimes there can be a price to pay if you're not "educated" on the storm of the day.

THE ANATOMY OF ONLINE MOBS

The internet has given everyone a voice, and that's both a blessing and a curse. On one side, it promotes the democratic sharing of thoughts and ideas. On the other, it can amplify and spread collective outrage, often devoid of nuance and understanding. With the click of a button, a single sentiment can snowball, gathering momentum and followers, until it becomes an unstoppable force.

Emotions, especially *fiery* ones like outrage and resentment, have a powerful *hook*.

Serena, an up-and-coming writer I worked with one summer, found herself trapped in a maze of fear, second-guessing every word she penned. Her platform had grown significantly over the years, offering insights on various social issues, culture, and personal growth. With a touch of appropriate humor woven into her work, she was hands down one of the most brilliant writers I'd come across. The words she wrote were once her sanctuary, but now they had become her prison.

The online world, which was a daily necessity for her work, buzzed with opinions, judgments, and digital trials. The place she'd found solace in was providing a platform for underrepresented voices, but it was also serving as a judge and jury for perceived wrongs. People were walking on eggshells, fearful of being misunderstood, misrepresented, or having past words dug up and used against them. Serena had always prided herself on her ability to communicate thoughtfully and empathetically, considering diverse perspectives while staying true to her voice. But a recent incident had shaken her confidence.

She had written a piece about a controversial topic, "The Ethics of Surrogacy: Exploring the Complexities of Renting a Womb," carefully weighing her words, providing examples, and constructing a balanced argument. She wanted to address the ethical dilemmas surrounding surrogacy, including valid questions around exploitation, the commodification of women's bodies, and the rights of all parties involved. Shortly after publishing, the article went viral, not for the depth of thought but for a single phrase that had been misinterpreted by a vocal group. The backlash was immediate, and Serena found herself thrust into a storm of criticism and judgment.

Torn between defending herself and the fear of making things worse, she felt paralyzed. She hadn't meant to offend, but the world had already made up its mind. Her sanctuary had been breached, her words twisted, her intentions questioned. She took a break from writing, needing time to reflect on what had happened. Her online home, a place that once inspired her, now felt like a reminder of the pitfalls of choosing to speak up. Everything seemed to close in, the constant chatter echoing the voices of judgment and misunderstanding.

As days turned into weeks, Serena began to realize something profound: the fear that had gripped her was not just about the misinterpretation of her words, it was about the loss of control over something deeply personal—her thoughts and expression. She understood that in trying to please everyone and offend no one, she had ceded control over her own voice. In her attempt to be perfect in her communication, she had overlooked the very thing that made it human—the possibility of misunderstanding, the ever-changing nature of interpretation, the essence of individual thought.

A mutual friend introduced Serena to me around that time, knowing that I'd previously navigated the rocky terrain of online spaces, and helped people do the same. When we first sat down for coffee, I could see the weight of the past weeks heavy on her. As she began telling me her story, it became clear that she was trapped in a black-and-white mindset, common in online discourse, where things are often seen as either completely right or entirely wrong. To challenge this perspective and introduce her to a more nuanced *third* way of thinking, I asked her a provoking question: "Have you considered that maybe the real power in your voice lies in fiercely accepting that the 'disappointment' of others is *not yours* to hold?"

I put this question forward to shift her focus from the fear of judgment, and possible victimhood, to the recognizing of her own power, and being okay with pissing people off.

You see, in the digital age, with its flashing screens and lightning-fast judgments, we often forget the power of pausing, reflecting, and zooming out. How often do you find yourself caught in the endless cycle of affirmation and rejection, scrolling through comments looking for validation or feeling crushed by a single criticism?

The real power in your voice
lies in fiercely accepting that
the "disappointment" of
others is *not yours* to hold.

Taking inspiration from that conversation and many that followed, I've created a reflective exercise for you. While Serena's situation may be unique, the emotions she struggled with and the potential lessons to be collected are universal. Whether you're an online creator, an active social media user, or just someone who's curious about the intricacies of the digital world, this exercise can offer a fresh perspective on navigating your online identity. In our digital age, how you express yourself online is just as important as how you do it in person.

NAVIGATING YOUR DIGITAL EXPRESSION

This exercise will guide you through understanding and refining how you share your thoughts online, and help you prepare for any bumps in the road so you can stay connected to your most honest voice, even in a sea of digital opinions. You're not only preparing for potential criticism, you're seeing your relationship with the digital world for what it really is, checking in on your boundaries (more on these later in the book), and making sure you exist in online spaces in a way that's true to who you are. This first stage is about Awareness, not immediate transformation.

You're about to take a lovely introspective walk through your digital home, taking on the role of an observer. Don't feel pressured to unearth profound insights right now. This is about gently uncovering aspects of your digital life you may not have considered before. It's a chance to explore your inner world without judgment. If nothing concrete surfaces at first, that's okay—these exercises are meant to be revisited and reflected upon over time. Let's begin this exploratory walk with an open mind.

Step 1: The Foundation of Your Digital Identity
We'll start by building a foundation for your digital identity, moving toward a more in-depth analysis of your online behaviors

71

and perceptions. Start by describing yourself in a paragraph as you would in an online bio. This sets the groundwork for your perceived digital identity.

Step 2: Evaluating Your Online Presence

After laying the groundwork with your digital identity, you will get even more curious about how you present and interact online. This step is about reflecting on the dynamics of your digital expression and understanding the impact of your online presence. Use these questions to guide your reflection:

- **Digital Versus Reality:** Compare the paragraph you wrote to your offline self. Are there any aspects of your identity that you amplify, minimize, or leave out online? For example, do you emphasize your adventurous side online but rarely seek adventures in real life?
- **Your Digital Audience:** When you share something online, who do you imagine as your primary audience? Friends, strangers, colleagues, clients, or a mix?
- **Intention Versus Potential Reception:** Think about a topic you care deeply about. If you were to post about it, what message would you want to convey? How do you think different groups (friends, family, strangers) might perceive it?
- **Anticipating Misunderstandings:** Are there certain topics or ideas you avoid sharing online due to fear of misinterpretation? Perhaps due to their complexity or sensitivity, like political views or personal beliefs. Why?
- **Your Digital Sanctuary:** What platforms or online spaces feel safest for you to express yourself? Why do you feel a sense of security there?
- **Facing Criticism:** Imagine you've shared a heartfelt post, and it

receives a negative comment. How would you respond? Would you defend, delete, engage in dialogue, or ignore?

- **Your Boundaries:** What personal rules or boundaries do you currently have for online engagement, such as not engaging in political debates or limiting personal information shared?
- **Feedback Versus Trolling:** How would you tell the difference between constructive feedback and pure trolling, especially in sensitive situations?
- **Resonance over Popularity:** Would you prefer a post to resonate deeply with a few people or be "liked" superficially by many? Why?
- **Digital Detox:** How often do you take breaks from social media or online interactions? Reflect on how these breaks (or the lack thereof) impact your mental well-being.

Remember, the aim here isn't to appease everyone, but to express genuinely, be prepared for diverse responses, and maintain mental and emotional well-being in the process. We'll cover more specific how-tos in Part 3, but your success is dependent on you taking the time to answer these questions and knowing your story.

Slowly, Serena began to write again, but with a renewed understanding. She accepted that she could not control how her message was received, only how it was delivered. She knew that the world was diverse and that her words would be seen through different lenses, colored by individual experiences and beliefs. Her writing took on a new dimension, one of courageous authenticity. She continued to strive for clarity, balance, and empathy, but she also embraced the risk of misinterpretation as an inherent part of human communication.

She engaged with her readers, opening avenues for dialogue and clarification, humanizing the process of communication. The fear that had once shackled her turned into the courage to express herself, understanding that disagreement, misunderstanding, or even offense might be the price she paid for voicing her thoughts.

Serena's platform grew not just in numbers but in the richness of conversation. Her readers appreciated her honesty and her refusal to let fear dictate her message. Her online world, once a symbol of her confinement, became a reminder of her liberation. She walked its streets with a renewed sense of purpose, her words not just a means of communication but a testament to the inherent value of telling the truth.

In a world where words were a minefield, she'd found a way to walk on them with grace, understanding, and courage. Her journey reflected a shared endeavor, a dance between speaker and listener, where the responsibility was mutual and the rewards profound. The fear of misinterpretation still lingered, but the fear of the mob no longer controlled her. It had become a reminder, a guide, a part of the human experience of sharing and connecting.

PROJECTION IN THE DIGITAL REALM

When you're scrolling through your social media feed and come across a comment that seems aggressive, without the benefit of facial cues or tone, your mind races to fill in the gaps. Is the commenter being sarcastic? Are they angry or just making a playful jest? In these split-second moments, it's all too easy to project your own feelings, past experiences, or fears onto the intentions of the commenter. This is the crux of online projection: the act of overlaying our personal emotions and biases onto digital interactions, often without even realizing it. But why is the online space such fertile ground for this phenomenon? There are three key reasons that come to mind…

- **Anonymity:** Online platforms make it easy for us to hide behind usernames and faceless profiles. While this anonymity can be liberating, it can also embolden some of the worst parts of humanity. Yes, it can bring out the worst in even the loveliest people. Free from direct consequences, it's not unusual for people to lead with their deepest fears, insecurities, and prejudices. Without others knowing who they are, they say things they'd normally keep to themselves, often making them sound louder and more intense than they meant to.

- **The Misleading Silence of Text:** In face-to-face interactions, you can see someone's facial expressions or hear their tone, helping you to get their real meaning. But online, without those nonverbal cues, it's easy to misunderstand a comment or message. A simple phrase can take on multiple shades of meaning, and your mindset at that moment can color your interpretation. It can be the decider of whether you react impulsively or respond from a grounded place. It's like looking at a silhouette in dim light: the shape is clear, but the details are left to your imagination.

- **Echo Chambers:** When algorithms constantly feed you content that aligns with your beliefs or triggers strong feelings, you find yourself in an echo chamber where you mainly hear the same opinion bounced back at you. Opposing views are rare, and maybe even unwelcome. After a while, you might think, "This is how everyone thinks!" or "This is the right way to think!" When a different opinion comes along, it feels wrong, even bad, so you might stop sharing some of your own thoughts to avoid any trouble or because you don't want to upset anyone. Even though the internet is so big, we can still end up in these small bubbles where everyone seems to think the same way. And in these bubbles, a single idea or worry can spread and grow until it's all anyone talks about.

I've been on both sides of this digital spectrum, and it's not a vantage point I'm proud of. But we're here to tell the truth, right? The year was 2020, a summer fraught with its own set of global challenges. This was the year I was shown just how deep I was in my own echo chamber. While the world outside battled with a pandemic, my internal world was grappling with a revelation that shook me to my core, one intertwined with the global outpouring of emotions after the tragic death of George Floyd. The Black Lives Matter (BLM) movement was raising awareness like never before, bringing critical issues of racial injustice and police brutality to the forefront in a way that was both powerful and transformative on a global scale. The movement sparked meaningful, timely, and very uncomfortable discussions, policy changes, and a broader understanding of systemic racism, which of course contributed significantly to social awareness and justice. As with many movements that start off well-intentioned, there were also some shadowy aspects. Reports would later come out of mismanagement of funds within the organization and accusations of misleading the public on certain issues that led to confusion among loyal followers, myself included. These controversies sparked discussions about transparency, accountability, and the complexities that often come with movements with such significant societal impact. But before this came to light, I found myself intensely drawn into the cause, passionately believing in its significance.

Remember Blackout Tuesday? I was one of those urging—no, demanding—people on my social media feed to speak up. My anger felt righteous. And looking back, I still empathize with that part of myself that wanted desperately for everyone to stand up against racial injustice. But I was blind in my intensity, failing to consider the many personal and varied reasons why someone might choose to remain silent or express their support differently. There I was, tapping away, adding my voice to the chorus of judgments, assumptions, and accusations, unaware of the echo I was amplifying.

It's a tough pill to swallow when you realize that the very thing you critique—the wave of uncontrolled emotion and the hive mind—is something you've been a part of. My participation wasn't passive; even though it was brief, I was active, vocal, and fiercely opinionated.

The comfort of being one in a sea of many voices, the thrill of rallying behind a cause so important, and the ease of hitting "send" before truly processing my thoughts—all this created a bubble of detachment from the consequences of my words. I'd become intoxicated by the rush of collective outrage without taking a moment to reflect on the broader implications and the individual journeys of those I was hastily judging.

The reckoning was swift. In one profound moment, the weight of my online actions smacked me in the face, and I found myself writing what would later become my open letter, unsubscribing from my own self-righteousness and ignorance. I needed to own up, not just for my sake, but as a testament to the countless others who've mindlessly scrolled, typed, and commented without grasping the ripple effect of their digital footprints. My intentions and messages, no matter how sincere, were exposed to the wide expanse of the internet, open to misinterpretation, judgment, and diverse perspectives. It was a humbling experience, to say the least. And it quickly broke me out of my online echo chambers, something I'm truly grateful for.

WHEN DIGITAL WORLDS COLLIDE

My "awakening" of sorts introduced me to a term I had never heard of before: context collapse. Defined simply, it's when different worlds collide. Instead of talking to specific groups separately like we used to, now it feels like we're speaking to one huge, mixed audience all at once. It's like trying to tell your best friend a secret, make your family laugh with a joke, and present a report to your boss, all at the same time, in the same room. Everyone's listening at once, and it's hard to know who you're really speaking to:

- **The Birthday Post:** Imagine sharing a candid birthday photo on a social media platform. To you, it's a nostalgic throwback to a fantastic (maybe slightly wild) night with close friends. But what happens when your work colleague, who only knows the professional side of you, stumbles upon it? Or when a distant family member decides to use that photo to comment on your life choices? The image was never intended for such diverse interpretations, but online, it's open season.

- **Political Opinions:** Drawing from my personal experience, sharing thoughts on the BLM movement seemed, to me, like expressing an essential human rights standpoint. But, in the digital realm, this view was suddenly open to scrutiny from every angle. The high school friend who grew up in a conservative household, the cousin from a different country with limited knowledge about American racial dynamics, and the colleague who might've had an entirely different racial experience—they were all on my "friends" list. To some, I was an activist; to others, perhaps misinformed or overly passionate. The context of my experiences and emotions collapsed under the weight of diverse interpretations.

- **A Casual Post:** You post a humorous observation about a popular TV show, expecting laughs or agreement from fellow fans. But someone shares it and, suddenly, people unfamiliar with the show's nuances are questioning your sense of humor, labeling it problematic, or insinuating things about your character.

- **Sharing a Memory:** Let's say you share a childhood photo of yourself and a friend wearing costumes from a cultural festival. For those who understand, it's a cherished memory. But for outsiders unfamiliar with the cultural context, it might appear as cultural appropriation, leading to unexpected backlash.

- **Professional Versus Personal:** LinkedIn is primarily a space for professional networking. But what if you share an article or thought piece about mental health and its impact on work productivity? While many would find it insightful, a potential employer might interpret it as you disclosing personal struggles, potentially affecting your job prospects.

If we're aware that our online "rooms" have blended together, we can be more thoughtful about what we share.

Each digital platform was once a room of its own, with its own rules, ambience, and guests. But, as I mentioned earlier, as our digital footprints have spread and audiences overlap, the walls between these rooms have become see-through. We're no longer speaking to our colleagues, friends, or family separately. We're speaking to them all at once, often without even realizing it. And once you post, you can't always control how people will take it. But if we're aware that our online "rooms" have blended together, we can be more thoughtful about what we share.

Understanding this new digital reality is one thing; navigating it is another. It's like standing at the center of a grand ballroom, acutely aware that your voice echoes to every corner, reaching friends, colleagues, and acquaintances alike. How do you maintain your authenticity while respecting the diverse audience in the room? It's a delicate balance, but it's achievable.

To help you unravel the complexities of this "context collapse" and find your footing in this expansive ballroom, I'll guide you through the following Unraveling Context Collapse exercise. It's one of my favorite tools to use with clients because it gives valuable insight into your digital presence. It will help you to become aware of the different "audiences" you interact with online and recognize the challenges and opportunities of overlapping contexts. If you take the time to think deeply as you go through each step, you will understand the overlapping worlds you're a part of, and learn how to communicate with intention and clarity. Even if you have fifty "followers," give this exercise your time and attention. Ready?

UNRAVELING CONTEXT COLLAPSE

Step 1: Identify Your Digital Spaces
List all the digital platforms you use regularly (e.g., Facebook, X, LinkedIn, Instagram).

Step 2: Define the Audience

For each platform, jot down the primary audiences you believe you're interacting with. For instance, LinkedIn might be "professional colleagues," Instagram might be "friends and followers," and so on.

Step 3: Recall and Reflect

Think of a recent post, comment, or share on each platform. Who were you thinking of when you posted it? Was it for a specific group, a close friend, the general public, or maybe just for yourself?

Step 4: Contextual Overlaps

Identify any instances where your content might have reached unintended audiences. Did your boss see holiday photos you shared with friends? Did a family member comment on a professional achievement meant for colleagues? Reflect on how this made you feel.

Step 5: Mindful Posting

Before posting something that might get a reaction from people, pause for a moment. Note I said pause, not overthink—remember, you're simply checking in with *you*—and curiously ask yourself:

- How would this post be perceived by different groups of people in my life?
- Are there any potential misunderstandings or misinterpretations?
- Am I okay with everyone on this platform seeing this?

Step 6: Adjust and Engage

Based on your reflections:

- Consider adjusting your privacy settings to better control who sees your content.
- Engage with your audience. If you post something meant for a specific group, maybe add a line or two explaining the context to others.

Step 7: Journal Your Insights

At the end of a week, take note of any changes in how you feel about your online interactions. Are you more comfortable? More authentic? Less stressed about potential overlaps?

When you reflect on the concept of context collapse and become more intentional and mindful about your online presence, you're essentially practicing the core principles of The Third Perspective—you're acknowledging the diversity of contexts, perspectives, and backgrounds that come together in the digital space. This approach is more than a lesson in online etiquette; it's an exercise in recognizing and respecting our shared humanity. You also give yourself a better shot at walking this virtual tightrope with grace and wisdom.

My personal story from the summer of 2020 is a case in point. Sharing this experience isn't about getting a pat on the back or seeking comfort. Instead, I share it because, like many of us, I, too, have been swept up in the digital current. What's important is reminding each other that we can hit "pause," think, and maybe take a different road. This is where the pillar of Awareness becomes your friend. It encourages you to step back, assess your actions and their impacts, and consider if there might be a more thoughtful, empathetic way to engage online, and offline.

With The Third Perspective, every action, whether it's a comment, a like, or a share, is seen as a contribution to a larger narrative. Each of us has the power to shape this collective story. Why not make your part of the story about challenging norms, sparking thoughtful debates, and building bridges where divides exist? Decide, now in this moment, that you'll commit to creating a narrative that doesn't cater to echoing popular opinions, but one that questions, learns, and grows. Use your digital platforms not just as echo chambers, but as stages for meaningful discourse and genuine connection. It's time to turn your online spaces into arenas of intellectual courage and compassionate dialogue. If you use your platforms more privately than others, keep in mind that this is not about making a big show, it's about changing your internal world, which will eventually reflect itself outside.

As we head into our next chapter, "Break Free from Either–Or Thinking," take this as your invitation to think broader, to see more, and to keep your curious mind open to the richness that lies beyond the obvious.

Chapter 5

Break Free from "Either–Or" Thinking

I t often feels as though we are living within the walls of a binary system. The internet, the media, and our social circles all seem to demand clear-cut stances on every issue. Are you left or right, pro or anti, with us or against us? This "either–or" mindset offers a sense of clarity, a quick fix, in a world overflowing with information and diverse perspectives. But is the world really as black and white as it's painted? The short answer is NO. As I hope you're coming to realize, the world you and I exist in is much more ambiguous than our brains and the surrounding noise would have us think. As I write these words in a small Portuguese village, there's a whirlwind of chaos brewing on social media. A violent political conflict rages in the Middle East, and it seems like everyone, regardless of where they are in the world, is expected to be intimately informed and to take a public stance. It's as if being on "the right side of history" is a badge everyone must wear, even if I were a shepherd in rural Gweru, Zimbabwe, far removed from the conflict itself, and probably facing one in my own country. The pressure to adopt and express the "correct" opinion, one that aligns with the perceived moral high ground, is immense and unforgiving.

This type of binary thinking ignores the plentiful reasons why people might not be as vocal or the various ways they might be contributing—from peaceful protests and writing to officials, to making donations or learning about the historical context they were previously unaware of. The assumption is that if you're not speaking or posting online, you're not doing anything at all. "Pics or it didn't happen" is in full force.

Like the pages of a printed book, once an opinion is declared when you lead with a fixed mindset, it seems to be permanent, unchangeable. However, this rigidity doesn't honor the nature of human growth and understanding. Your perspectives should be fluid, evolving as you do, and as the world around you changes. Sticking to a strict "this-or-that" mentality is like clinging to an outdated story that no longer represents your current reality. You need the freedom to learn, evolve, and appreciate the vast array of thoughts and views life offers. You need to give yourself permission to step away from the limiting and outdated trap of binary thinking.

If I hadn't gone through my experience back in 2020, which we explored in the previous chapter, I know that I, too, would be caving under the pressure most people feel when a horrific worldly event happens and spills onto their social feeds. I have received hundreds of DMs and emails in the past week from people struggling to know how to respond, and whether they should post something, anything, so that it quiets the noise. I deeply empathize and honor the part of us that sees injustice and wants people to do something about it immediately. But with the globalization of technology, it can be easy to assume that someone not posting or advocating loudly on social media means they don't care about said issue. This thinking disconnects us from each other and stops us from unifying, finding effective solutions, advocating, and effecting change. Instead, it keeps us afraid, anxious, and frustrated. Because it seems that there is no getting it right.

In this chapter, we'll be focusing on how we can begin to change that. I'm hopeful we can start contributing, in our own ways, to shaping a society that sees the full spectrum of life—a society that openly embraces and encourages The Third Perspective.

With the globalization of technology, it can be easy to assume that someone not posting or advocating loudly on social media means they don't care about said issue.

APPRECIATING AMBIGUITY

I invite you to think of ambiguity as being like the color gray in a world that demands you pick between black and white. It's the "maybe," the "I don't know," the "it depends," in a world that says you need to give a confident "yes" or "no" at the drop of a hat. I know that you may run into the fear of being labeled indecisive, ignorant, shallow, unreflective, or wishy-washy, which makes it tougher to embrace ambiguity. But what if I told you that your power lies exactly there, in your ability to sit comfortably with uncertainty?

This doesn't mean that there aren't moments that call for clear-cut stances. I have my own strong beliefs. You might think I'm contradicting myself here, but, for me, there are certain areas where black-and-white thinking is not just acceptable, but necessary. For instance, when it comes to fundamental human rights, my stance is unwavering. On this, I won't budge. Everyone deserves fair treatment, without exception. So, in the face of grave injustices like torture, child labor, racism, sexism, hate crimes, or any violation of basic human dignity, there is no room for ambiguity. In these cases, I'll always speak up against these atrocities and my speaking up doesn't equate to social media being my default. While I don't expect everyone to fight these battles the same way I do, I believe it's crucial to raise awareness and get the word out in effective ways.

Even with these nonnegotiables, I try to think critically and carefully about how I respond. I always strive to not react solely based on emotion, even though it's hard to not just go with your gut reaction. Over the years I've learned just how important it is to engage with these issues thoughtfully, not impulsively, even when the emotional pull is incredibly strong. That means I do my absolute best to keep a balance—feeling strongly, but also thinking things through. It's all about channeling that energy in ways that really count, so that what I do and say really makes a difference. This commitment to a mindful response, even in the face of clear-cut wrongs, shows how much thoughtful action matters in everything, especially when it comes to things that hit hard on the ideas of "right" and "wrong." And believe me, I know how tough it can be.

I hope this highlights how important it is to stand strong. But, even when you do, you should remember to see the individual stories and situations, and try with all your might to approach them with care and compassion.

The examples I previously mentioned are extremes in the sense that you might not be encountering these situations on a daily basis, and it's in these extreme cases that we should all be able to apply common sense. This book focuses on your daily life—your everyday interactions, both online and offline. As we move forward, let's not let our minds leap to extremes. We're talking about the nuances in the conversations you have every day, the posts you scroll past or engage with, the discussions that challenge you and the ones that affirm you. This is about finding balance and perspective in the fabric of your everyday life.

I want you to know that appreciating ambiguity is like being a skilled musician. You understand that every note has its place in the composition, but also that not all notes should be played at the same time. You recognize that sometimes a strong, clear note is needed to cut through the silence, while at other times, a softer, more subtle note is appropriate. The music is richer, fuller, and more nuanced because of your ability to distinguish and apply these differences.

When you're comfortable with the grays of life, you take your time to weigh up the different perspectives, to question, to reflect, and to form an opinion that aligns with your values (which we'll uncover in Part 2). You're not in a rush to fit in or conform. You're willing to dive deep, to question the norms, and to explore the different shades available to you. I find this to be a very liberating and grounding mindset to move through the world with. Navigating ambiguity in a culture of fear and intolerance isn't about being indecisive or not taking a stand. It's about taking a pause instead of rushing to conclusions or making hasty judgments. It's about giving yourself the space to understand, to question, and to learn before forming an opinion. It's about not letting fear push you into a corner, but rather using your personal principles as your guiding light.

In practice, this can look like taking a step back when presented with a controversial issue. Instead of jumping on the bandwagon, it means taking your time to gather information, to understand different perspectives, and to question your own preconceived notions. It means not feeling the need to immediately respond or react when someone challenges your viewpoint, but rather allowing yourself the space to reflect and perhaps change your mind.

Walk out into the world with the *knowledge* that you're not a puppet to be swayed by the winds of public opinion. You're a person with your own unique set of values, experiences, and perspectives. Give yourself permission to explore, to learn, and to walk the path less traveled. True self-expression isn't about conforming; it's about allowing yourself to shine distinctively, on your own terms. In a world obsessed with clear-cut black and white, dare to embrace the shades of gray. In a world that loves binary, be a proud inhabitant of the gray area. This is where the real magic happens—in the nuanced dance with ambiguity. This is where you'll find freedom from the chains of fear and the boldness to uphold your values, regardless of their popularity (you'll define these in the next chapter). It's in these shades of gray that you learn the beauty of uncertainty, the power of questioning (keep asking!), and the importance of evolving.

With this concept in mind, let's not just leave it at words. How about we put this into practice? Right here, right now. I've got a little thought experiment for you. Nothing too daunting, I promise—just a few reflective prompts to get those cognitive gears turning.

Walk out into the world with the *knowledge* that you're not a puppet to be swayed by the winds of public opinion.

SHADES OF GRAY

Step 1: Black-and-White Scenario

Think of a recent issue or event where you felt a strong pull toward a "black-or-white" viewpoint. What was the topic? How did you feel about it?

Step 2: Information Source

Where did your initial information come from? Was it a single source or multiple? Did you feel the source(s) was biased in any way?

Step 3: Embracing the Gray

Try to identify three "gray" or middle-ground perspectives related to that issue. These don't need to be viewpoints you agree with, but aim to understand them.

Step 4: Personal Reaction

Reflect on a moment when you felt pressured to conform to a certain stance or opinion because of peers, social media, or society. How did that make you feel? Did it align with your genuine beliefs?

Step 5: Moving Forward

How can you approach the next divisive issue with a more open, "shades of gray" mindset? What steps will you take to ensure you're making a considered, rather than reactive, judgment?

By spending some time on these questions, you'll begin to see the spectrum of perspectives available and you can place value in seeking out and understanding multiple viewpoints before solidifying your own stance. It'll not only help you become a better communicator, but a better critical thinker!

THE QUIET ADVANTAGES OF SITTING ON THE SIDELINES (WITHOUT UNPACKING YOUR SUITCASE THERE!)

People might want you to pick a side. And if you don't? It can sometimes earn you an undeserved label: a "fence-sitter." Some may even say you can't make up your mind or that you don't really care about the issue. They may frame it as a lack of conviction in anything. But that's not true. Choosing to see the bigger picture isn't about avoiding choices. Standing in the middle and seeing both sides? That takes courage.

Consider the term "fence-sitter" for a second. On the surface, it paints an image of someone teetering, scared to lean too far in one direction. It evokes the idea of remaining frozen in a state of indecision. This picture is wrong. People who embrace the gray areas aren't just mindlessly hanging out on fences—they're building bridges. They're connecting different ideas and perspectives, and seeing the bigger picture.

Say one of your close friends wholeheartedly believes in unrestricted free speech, saying every voice must be heard without censorship. Another emphasizes the dangers of hate speech and the real-world harms it can cause to vulnerable groups. You see merit in both arguments. You advocate for free speech but also support clear boundaries on speech that incites violence or poses immediate harm. Or think about the heated immigration debates you might hear around the dinner table or on TV. Some people are worried about job losses or safety, wanting tight borders. Others highlight the stories of refugees in need or talk about how different cultures make our country richer. You understand the fears and the ideals on both sides. Instead of just backing one team, you're saying, "Why not find a way that keeps us safe and also helps those in need?" You're not sitting on the sidelines; you're looking for a balanced, caring approach that works for everyone.

Living in the gray area, acknowledging nuance, does not mean you are unwilling to take a stand. A lot of the time, it takes guts. It means you're brave enough to say, "Hey, this stuff is complicated." It's about wanting to get the full story, not just the headlines. You're not just going for the easy answer; instead, you're taking the time to really get it, to see the full picture. That's not being wishy-washy; it's being thoughtful. You're not unsure; you just want to make sure you've got it right. And even if you are unsure, owning up to that allows you to practice intellectual integrity.

The next time someone accuses you of "sitting on the fence," remind yourself that you're not sitting at all. You're firmly moving along your path, guided by your supportive beliefs and your commitment to staying open. Refuse to let the labels people place on you discourage you. Keep *exploring*, keep *questioning*, and keep *growing*. The path you're walking on is not one that doesn't have conviction; it's just that the convictions you stand for are of a different nature. In today's society, there's a palpable pressure to have 100 percent conviction in your thoughts and opinions—it's as if there's no room for doubt or questioning. This expectation can be paralyzing, and it's a big reason why people are scared into silence for fear of not appearing fully certain or committed to a viewpoint that is seen as "correct." But your convictions don't have to lean on black-and-white simplicity, but rather on the appreciation of complexity. This path involves embracing the discomfort that comes with not always being completely sure. This discomfort, though unsettling, is fertile ground for growth and learning. You will need to accept that true strength lies in the ability to sit with uncertainty, to be comfortable with not always having a definitive stance, and to allow your thoughts and beliefs the space to evolve. You're not lost; you're just open to seeing things in more ways than one. To really embody this mindset, you need to accept that being open-minded isn't being weak—it's about knowing there's always more to the story.

Your goal here is not to please the crowd or to avoid making tough decisions. Your goal is to become more thoughtful and considerate before being swept away by the power of reaction. This takes time,

Refuse to let the labels
people place on you
discourage you. Keep
exploring, keep *questioning*,
and keep *growing*.

patience, and practice, but the outcome is worth it. As you grow more comfortable wading in the waters of ambiguity, you become more resilient, adaptable, and empathetic. So, continue to appreciate those gray areas, the in-betweens, the spaces that don't fit neatly within defined boundaries. As you do, you'll discover that these spaces are not empty or meaningless, but filled with insights and possibilities that are waiting to be explored. Embrace it all and, remember, your convictions are not lost in this process, they're enriched.

BEYOND LABELS: IDENTITY IN A BINARY WORLD

During an intimate fireside chat at a literary festival, a famous author known for his charity work and forward-thinking views found himself in a tricky spot. He was asked about his thoughts on a new policy being introduced into the publishing world, one that had deeply divided opinions—the new policy aimed at enforcing an "author identity verification." This would require authors, especially those writing about marginalized or underrepresented groups, to verify their identity and background. The idea was to stop writers from borrowing other cultures' stories without truly understanding them. They wanted to prevent "cultural appropriation." Some said it was about giving a proper platform to those often overlooked voices. Others thought it would limit creativity, amplify identity politics, and might even lead to unintentional segregation in literature.

People were caught off guard by his response. Many assumed he would think a certain way because he's Black. But instead of just going along with the popular view, he had a more balanced take. He said, "I get why this rule is there—to support voices that often go unheard. But stories connect us all. I worry this rule might acciden-tally box in stories to just one type of background. Stories are where we feel for others. A writer from one place can touch a reader from somewhere else. We need to be careful about borrowing from other cultures, but that doesn't mean stories only belong to one group. Just because I'm Black doesn't mean I can only write about Black lives. That limits creativity. And people from other backgrounds can get the Black experience if they really try and are respectful."

The room started buzzing, social media went wild, and the next day's news had big headlines about him turning his back on his own community. People began doubting if he was really on their side, and some even wanted to stop buying his books. "Wasn't he one of us?" some lamented. Yet, in his quiet reflection, he asked: "Can't I agree with some things and disagree with others?" The very tags and labels that once made him feel part of a group now boxed him in. And when he stepped out of that box, the fallout was swift and unforgiving.

We all like that feeling of being part of a group, right? It's like that silent agreement, those shared moments and common ideas that make us feel at home. It's like we're all on the same team. It's as if we're all leaves on the same branch, swaying to the rhythm of a shared wind. But what happens when you feel like you're dancing to a different tune than everyone else?

"Who am I?" is the question that tends to step to the forefront. It's one of the oldest and most profound questions we ask ourselves. And in our search for answers, we often find comfort in labels. We proudly wear these tags: Democrat or Republican, conservative or liberal, religious or atheist, traditionalist or progressive. These identity markers give us a sense of belonging, a tribe we can align with, and a road map for our beliefs and actions. Which is useful, beautiful even, and inherently human. But what if these groups or labels start to feel too tight? What if they stop you from thinking freely or growing as a person? The answer, dear reader, may not be easy to digest.

If you've built your identity around being a "liberal," for example, it can be uncomfortable, even scary, to entertain thoughts that seem "conservative." I've been there, turning away from different ideas because I was worried that just trying to understand them would make me "right-wing," which felt like being on the wrong side. Today, when everything gets politicized, it's easy to stick to ideas that seem more accepted by society. But, think about complex topics like the sex industry, the explosion of online platforms selling explicit sexual content, the different sides of porn, or the many waves of feminism. These topics can really puzzle even those who are usually very open-minded.

Take the sex industry—it's a real challenge for liberal views. It raises big questions about personal choice, exploitation, and morality. Where do we draw the line between self-empowerment and being objectified? And porn? It's caught between being free to express and possibly spreading harmful ideas.

Feminism itself has lots of different ideas and doesn't always agree on these issues. How do we support sex workers while critiquing the industries they're in? How do liberal ideals fit with making money off sexuality? Can you see how fear of betraying your self-proclaimed identity or, worse, being cast out by your tribe, often leads to self-censorship? It's important to know that trying to understand these complicated issues doesn't mean you're giving up on what you believe.

It's not about labeling things as simply good or bad, but about seeing all the different sides they have. It might feel uncomfortable, but it's necessary to really get the whole picture. The world isn't just black and white—it's full of different colors and perspectives. Your job is to try to understand, not just put a label on everything, and to think about these things in a way that's both careful and caring.

The topic of identity gets even more interesting because it's not just about differing opinions. The very notion of *who* gets to voice an opinion on certain topics depends a lot on what identity the person holds, especially in modern society. Maybe you've found yourself questioning whether you "qualify" to contribute to a conversation because you didn't have the "right" identity? Believe it or not, in modern society, this is a fear many people have. And this fear of crossing invisible boundaries can make you retreat into silence.

Let's take a moment to understand the labels that define your daily life, how they guide your actions, and where they might conflict or align.

IDENTITY WEB: UNTANGLING THE THREADS OF SELF

Spend a few minutes on each following question. Critically assess them and write down your thoughts or discuss them with someone you trust. The goal here is to stimulate self-reflection and deeper understanding of your identity beyond the constraints of labels.

- Can you recall a moment when you resisted one of your self-imposed labels? How did it feel?
- Are there any labels you've outgrown but still cling to out of habit or societal pressure?
- Think about a label or identity you're proud of. Would you feel differently about yourself if it were removed? Why or why not?
- Have you ever hesitated to voice an opinion because it didn't align with one of your labels or the perceived viewpoint of that label?
- If you could introduce yourself without using any typical labels (like job titles, racial or ethnic identifiers, and so on), how would you describe who you are?
- How do you think people without knowledge of your labels perceive you? Does that differ from how you perceive yourself?
- Do your labels empower you or confine you more? Can they do both?

Having thought about the questions in the aforementioned exercise, it's essential to remember that labels and identities, while valuable, are just one aspect of the multifaceted gem that is you. They can provide a sense of belonging and understanding, but they shouldn't confine or limit your growth. Allow yourself to evolve, to challenge, and to expand beyond the boundaries set by society or even by yourself.

REVISITING SELF-CENSORSHIP

So, we've been on quite a journey, right? From the tribal days of our ancient ancestors to the inner workings of our brains, and right up to the challenges of modern communication. Each of these chapters in your story has added layers, influencing how you choose to share your voice. You've unpacked a lot about who you are, how you change, and the boxes society sometimes tries to put you in. I myself have reflected on a lot as I've been walking alongside you in these pages. Be it school-yard memories, the fear of not fitting in, the desire to stand out—all of it plays a part. This exploration of identity, open-mindedness, and the world around us naturally brings us back to our central theme: self-censorship, our silent gatekeeper.

As we wrap up Part 1, it's crucial for you to gauge the current role of self-censorship in your life. Have our recent explorations changed how you view it? Or how you practice it? I designed the following exercise to help you spotlight your own patterns of expression. And now that you're probably a little more comfortable with going inward, I trust that you will answer honestly.

This Self-Silencing Scale is for all of us—to see where we stand in the vast spectrum of communication before moving on to the next pillar: Responsibility. Whether you're someone who shies away from sharing their opinion or someone who dives headfirst into every debate, this exercise aims to refine your approach. Will it help you understand yourself? Yes. And will it also help you understand other people? Absolutely!

THE SELF-SILENCING SCALE

For each following statement, rate how often it is true for you on a scale from 1 to 5, with 1 being "Never" and 5 being "Always." Consider everything you've learned about moving beyond binary thinking, understanding the complexities of situations, and the role your identity plays in your communication. Focus mainly on what's been happening lately, but also think back to the past if it helps you see a pattern in how you usually behave. Remember, we are trying to pinpoint your habitual or default responses, rather than isolated incidents. This consistent reflection will ensure a more accurate score. Don't overthink it—answer honestly and intuitively.

- I hold my tongue, even when I'm bursting with a differing opinion.
- Group dynamics often overshadow my desire to voice my true feelings.
- Before sharing online, I excessively scrutinize my words, fearing potential criticism.
- For me, peace in conversations often comes at the cost of my authentic voice.
- There are moments when I witness something I feel is wrong, yet choose silence over confrontation.
- To prevent ruffling feathers, I sometimes dilute my feedback, even if it's constructive.
- I've let someone take credit for my idea because speaking up seemed daunting.
- I've doubted the validity of my own experiences because they differed from the majority.
- I've dimmed my accomplishments to avoid appearing boastful.
- In my close relationships, I've suppressed my feelings to keep the peace.

- I've altered my physical appearance or behavior to fit in with a group.
- I've avoided discussions on certain topics because they felt "too controversial."
- I feel nervous about discussing topics I'm passionate about, fearing I might be seen as "too much."
- I've not corrected someone when they assumed something incorrect about me, to avoid a scene.
- My needs often fade into the background, making way for others' preferences.

Scoring

15–30: Low: You tend to speak your mind and are comfortable in most situations. Yet, a closer lens might reveal areas where refining your social filter could be beneficial.

31–45: Moderate: You sometimes hold back based on the situation. It will be worth exploring what triggers these moments of silence. Are they always necessary or are they based on unfounded fears?

46–60: High: You frequently suppress your voice and prioritize others' feelings or perceptions over your own thoughts and feelings.

61–75: Very High: Almost always, you're holding back. Recognize this pattern and understand that your voice is valuable.

By taking part in this exercise, you're not only assessing your patterns, but are actively choosing to confront them. This is where the good stuff lies. The results might surprise you, affirm what you already know, or shed light on unnoticed tendencies. Whichever it is, this introspective exploration is a great way to set the foundation for the next pillar, as we unravel the threads of what it looks like for you to express yourself bravely, regardless of external happenings.

Now, take a deep breath.

Reflect on the score you wrote down from the Self-Silencing Scale exercise. It provides an introspective lens into how often you might mute your own voice, often in the service of avoiding conflict or maintaining relational harmony. That number is not a judgment but a signpost, marking where you stand right now and getting you prepared for what's next. Now, as we move into exploring Responsibility, you're going to learn about using your voice in a way that's both thoughtful and effective. This stage is all about striking that perfect balance. You will be speaking up in a manner that's genuine and aligns seamlessly with the core values you'll identify and firmly establish. You'll be taking the reins of your communication and making sure it mirrors what you truly stand for. This exploration is particularly vital in our current culture, which, as you know, tends to lean toward fear and a collective tendency to sabotage ourselves and others. By honing your ability to communicate responsibly, you'll walk even the fieriest of paths with greater ease and confidence. You'll be equipped to face situations where speaking up might seem daunting or where the pressure to conform threatens to overshadow your personal truths. I'm ready if you are.

PART 2

Responsibility:

WHAT DO YOU STAND FOR?

Welcome to the pillar of Responsibility. Your path is about to take a profound turn.

The foundational work you have done in Part 1 will allow you to zero in on aligning your voice's intention with its impact. You will do this by first focusing on your core values. These will be your anchors when external pressures might otherwise sway you. You will do more than simply *have* them; you will be living them and making sure that they trickle into every area of your communication and your life. Every conversation, even the ones with yourself. Every post. Every call. You'll see how this guiding system impacts how you connect with people, how you make decisions, and how you react to what happens around you.

Then, we'll figure out your communication style. Are you bold or more reserved? Do you lead with your heart or your head? Knowing this will help you understand how you connect with others and how to adjust your style in different situations without losing yourself. Your listening style is just as important. Are you really hearing what people say or just waiting for your turn to speak? We'll find out.

Next, we'll look at getting your talking and listening to work together. We want it to work *for* you. This is key to having real, meaningful conversations where everyone, including you, feels acknowledged and respected. Finally, we'll focus on building a strong self-reputation that lasts. This is about creating an image of yourself that you're proud of, one that stays solid no matter what others say or think. This is where you will take ownership of your words and actions.

Through this phase, expect a transformative experience as you ground yourself in the message of The Third Perspective. You'll cultivate a voice that's clear, impactful, and resonant, coupled with a listening ear that seeks to understand *before* being understood. I'm excited for you! This is all about taking ownership of your communication, refining it and making sure it truly represents who you are, and who you are becoming. Are you ready to take on the responsibility?

Chapter 6

Principles Worth Defending

You'll recall that you explored your beliefs in Chapter 2, but it's time to take it a step further—we're going to have an honest conversation about values, the core principles that guide your life. The ones you will be defending. Remember, though, beliefs and values, while closely linked, are not the same. Beliefs, when held tightly and without being reviewed from time to time, *evolve* into values.

Think of it this way: Your beliefs are like seeds you've planted and slowly nurtured over time. They are the starting point. As they face and survive life's relentless trials, they become deep-rooted and sturdy. This is where defining elements of who you are formed. Take, for example, a belief in open-mindedness, not just as a nice idea but as a radical approach to life, formed from your own eclectic experiences and an insatiable thirst for knowledge. You fiercely challenge yourself to consider perspectives that are worlds apart from your own, refusing to succumb to the comfort of echo chambers.

This openness becomes a key part of who you are in conversations. It means you're more likely to listen to and consider different viewpoints instead of just shutting down or editing what you really think. Or maybe you have a staunch belief in fairness, not the textbook kind, but a firebrand fairness born from your own confrontations with injustice. This belief isn't passive; it propels you to raise your voice when things aren't right, even if it means saying something that others might not agree with. While beliefs are your understanding of the world, values are the *nonnegotiable* standards you live by. They shape your decisions, your actions, and, ultimately, your character. And most of the time you won't even realize that they are leading you. Your value system becomes a well-oiled machine that runs without you even knowing.

In this chapter, you'll go beyond identifying what you believe; you'll pinpoint what you're willing to stand for, even when things get chaotic. It's about the moments when honesty, integrity, or courage aren't just ideas, but the ground you plant your feet on. This is where you find the courage to make choices that match with your deepest convictions, even when they challenge you or set you apart.

Our exploration will present you with some questions that need answering: What are the values I'm willing to uphold, no matter what? What principles are so ingrained in my being that they influence every significant choice I make? I'm not being dramatic, but the answers you'll get from these questions, and the actions you take following this, will shape your path and define your legacy.

This phase, Responsibility, is where things get real—and intense. It's often the most transformative and challenging part of the journey because this is where you get closer to pairing Awareness with action. Think about it: when you choose to speak up, take a stand, or dive into deep conversations, both in your private life and in the public eye, you're taking on a hefty load of responsibility. And let's be clear: it's not always going to be comfortable. Nor should it be. But this doesn't give you a free pass to be reckless or careless with your words. Responsibility is the bedrock of The Third Perspective— it's that way of thinking that pushes you beyond simple black-and-white views, into the rich, complex grays of life. It's about standing firm in what you believe in, while navigating the nuanced realities of the world.

While beliefs are your understanding of the world, values are the *nonnegotiable* standards you live by.

My own path wasn't exactly a straight road. During my days lost in a haze of blackout drinking, my choices were all about the next thrill, the next high, avoiding any pain and doing what felt good right then and there—without a thought for the consequences. Future Me was always left to deal with the aftermath. But as I boarded the sobriety train again (eighth time's the charm, right?), my real values—self-respect, responsibility, resilience in the face of adversity, forming genuine connections sans alcohol—came into sharp focus. Stepping bravely into these values was anything but easy. It was a jolt, a harsh wake-up call. There was no glossy Hollywood sheen to my story. It was raw, often brutal, mostly ugly, but it eventually got beautiful.

With each day that came, I chose a life in clarity. It didn't fall into my lap—I had to *choose* it and *work* for it. I started to see myself and the world around me differently. Witnessing this change in myself made me understand how powerful values really are, and it's something I hadn't given much thought to before. The values I had as a drinker (pleasure-seeking, avoidance, a desire to escape) compared to the ones I now held as a nondrinker were like night and day. In the past I'd have probably yawned at the word "values" because it brings to mind memories of forgettable corporate slogans. But what we're delving into here is far deeper, and certainly more memorable. Bottom line: when you don't know what you stand for, you will always be at the mercy of the external world. So, when I talk about having "principles worth defending," I'm referring to *your* core values—the foundation of who you are.

I want you to remember that owning your story, with all its rough edges, is where true strength lies. It's about embracing the hard truths, the tough lessons, and emerging with a set of convictions that are unshakably yours. This is not just about survival; it's about *thriving* in your truth.

When you don't know
what you stand for, you
will always be at the mercy
of the external world.

In 2013, Edward Snowden, a former CIA employee and NSA contractor, made headlines around the world when he leaked classified documents. He showed that big agencies, with help from phone companies and some other countries, were watching and storing a lot of our personal data. Snowden did this because he felt people had a right to know. He thought these agencies were going too far and stepping on our privacy rights. In simple words, he wanted everyone to know how much they were being watched. I get chills every time I think or write about his story. It's one of the most extraordinary stories that comes to mind when I think about someone audaciously committing to their values.

However, the US government viewed Snowden's actions as a betrayal, charging him with theft of government property and two counts under the Espionage Act. To avoid getting arrested, Snowden fled the United States, spending time in Hong Kong before being granted asylum in Russia, where he remains to this day.

Snowden's story shows the price someone might pay for staying true to their values. He sacrificed a nice comfortable life, a great paycheck, and the ability to live in his home country—all because he believed in transparency, privacy, and the public's right to know what was happening with their data. Despite the personal risks and the significant controversies around his decisions, Snowden's actions, with their worldwide implications, highlight the essence of The Third Perspective: the power of staying true to your core values, and being prepared to make hard calls to stay aligned with them. His commitment to truth and public awareness is a phenomenal example of how deeply personal choices, grounded in integrity, can ripple out to create significant global conversations and shifts. I have experienced and still continue to experience this firsthand. This is the heart of The Third Perspective: recognizing that your individual actions, especially when driven by unwavering values, can be catalysts for sparking far-reaching change—a change that has the power to happen on a global scale.

BENEFITS OF VALUES IN THE AGE OF
COLLECTIVE SABOTAGE AND SELF-CENSORSHIP

- **Grounding amid Chaos:** In a time of rapid change, where opinions fluctuate, knowing your values offers a steady anchor. It gives you a consistent base from which you can form opinions and take actions.
- **Authentic Expression:** With clear values, your expression becomes more genuine. Even when challenged, you can stand by your words knowing they're rooted in your *core* (chosen) beliefs.
- **Resilience to Criticism:** When you're clear on your values, external criticism can be taken constructively. You're less likely to be swayed by every opposing viewpoint or feel attacked personally.
- **Reduced Fear of Backlash:** Understanding and standing by your values may reduce the apprehension of speaking out, even in fear of collective sabotage. You can speak with conviction, knowing your standpoints are well-founded.
- **Enhanced Self-Esteem:** Acting in alignment with your values boosts confidence. You're not constantly second-guessing or feeling inauthentic, leading to a heightened sense of self-worth.
- **Building Trust:** Consistently acting from a place of value builds trust among peers and audiences. They know what to expect from you, and this consistency fosters credibility. But best of all, you deepen your self-trust.
- **Deeper Connections:** Sharing and living by your values can help you connect with like-minded individuals, which leads to deeper and more meaningful relationships. Sign me up!
- **Clarity in Uncertainty:** In situations where the "right" choice isn't clear, your values can illuminate the path, providing clarity in the face of uncertainty.

- **Empowerment Against Self-Censorship:** When you're firm in your values, the grip of self-censorship loosens. It really does. You feel empowered to share your perspectives without constantly self-editing or suppressing your voice.
- **Informed Decision-Making:** Knowing your values helps you make better decisions, especially when things get tricky. It allows you to weigh options and potential outcomes against your core values, leading to choices that are not just reactive, but reflective and well-considered. This way, you're not just reacting on the fly; you're thinking things through based on what's important to you. In a world where it's easy to make quick, impulsive decisions, this approach helps you stay grounded and make choices with real purpose.

IDENTIFYING YOUR VALUES

Consider Snowden. He made a pivotal choice because he believed in something so strongly. Now, most of us don't face such extremes, and I'm not expecting you to sacrifice your life as you know it (I'm going to assume that you're not holding government secrets or hiding from international espionage), but we all have moments when we have to decide between the straightforward and the morally correct. What's easy and what's right. We all come across moments that test our principles. Perhaps you've felt something off at work and needed to address it, or a moment with friends when you had to choose the harder right over the easier wrong, or felt the urge to voice your thoughts on societal events, despite the fear. I've been there (I find myself back here!)—at the intersection of comfort and conviction. Every time I've had to initiate a tough conversation, whether with a partner, family member, or client, there's a part of me that hesitates. And every time I decide to share a viewpoint I know might stir the pot, which is part of my daily work, I feel that familiar twinge

116

of apprehension. But, more powerful than my resistance is my commitment to honesty. It's about seizing these moments as opportunities for growth, instead of shying away from them.

Snowden's choices weren't just about the dramatic flair of whistleblowing; they were about staying true to his fundamental beliefs, regardless of the cost. And that's something we all face in less grandiose, but equally significant, ways. It's in these smaller, personal arenas where our values are truly tested and where we find out just how much we're willing to stand up for what we believe. So when you find yourself at one of these junctures, ask yourself: What's more important—the comfort of the status quo or the integrity of your values? When we cover risk a little bit later in the book, you'll be able to put all of this groundwork into perspective, but best of all, into action.

Now, examine the following list of values. Without overanalyzing, notice which ones deeply resonate with you:

- **Authenticity:** Being true to who you are and what you believe.
- **Courage:** Facing fears and tough situations head-on.
- **Integrity:** Doing what's right, even when it might not be popular.
- **Transparency:** Being clear and honest about what you think and feel.
- **Freedom:** Living life on your own terms, without unnecessary limits.
- **Boldness:** Daring to be different and take chances.
- **Respect:** Valuing everyone's opinions and rights, including your own.
- **Individuality:** Celebrating what makes you, you.
- **Resilience:** Bouncing back from tough times.
- **Self-Awareness:** Knowing your feelings, beliefs, strengths, and areas to grow.

- **Responsibility:** Owning up to what you do and believe.
- **Assertiveness:** Clearly saying what you need and want with confidence.
- **Liberation:** Breaking free from others' expectations.
- **Curiosity:** Being eager to learn and see things from different angles.

WHAT WE SAY VERSUS WHAT WE DO

Values are like personal compasses—they guide you, help you make choices, and show who you truly are. But, have you ever noticed a gap between the things you believe in and the way you act? Now that you've identified your values, let's explore that.

EMBODIED VALUES: IN ACTION

When we talk about embodied values, we're discussing the beliefs that genuinely drive your actions every day. These aren't just things you say you believe in, but what you *show* you believe in through your actions.

Example: Integrity

Being honest and upright is important to you. When you find yourself in a situation where you might gain something by stretching the truth a bit, you don't compromise on this value for a fleeting advantage. You stand by what you believe is right, even when no one is watching.

Example: Kindness

Even when it's a little inconvenient, you always choose kindness. You are not kind because you think you should be—it's just who you are. Your actions, no matter how big or small, consistently reflect a heart full of compassion and consideration for others.

Example: Authenticity

You genuinely believe in speaking your mind and, in various settings, you voice your opinions without giving in to self-censorship. Your behavior clearly shows an embodied value of authenticity, regardless of the potential pushback you might receive.

DESIRED VALUES: THE IDEALS WE STRIVE FOR

These are the values you admire and want to have—an aspiration. They're the ideals you respect, like honesty, hard work, and creativity. However, just because you respect these values doesn't mean you always act on them. Putting them into practice takes effort and, sometimes, a bit of compassionate self-checking.

Example: Ambition

Maybe you admire ambition. You love the idea of setting big goals and chasing dreams. You might even talk about your big plans for the future. But, when faced with an opportunity to put in extra hours or take a risk, you don't quite step up to the plate.

Example: Generosity

It's a value many cherish. Perhaps you often talk about wanting to give back, help others, and be charitable. But, when there's only one piece of pie left or a chance to donate some spare change, you prioritize holding back.

Example: Diversity of Thought

You may claim to value diverse perspectives and state that you're open to hearing all sides of a story. You admire people who can patiently sit through opinions they vehemently disagree with. However, in reality, you avoid such conversations or shut them down before they begin, thus displaying a gap between your desired value and your true action.

TIME FOR A QUICK CHECK-IN

Think about it. Do your actions match up with the values you talk about? I was astounded when I learned that a lot of the values I took as part of my identity were not actually embodied. They were mostly desired. I wanted to be more transparent, I wanted to value diversity of thought, I wanted to lead with integrity. But my actions, especially in the summer of 2020, showed me that I had embodied the values of conformity and safety at all costs. Realizing there might be a gap isn't about feeling guilty. I know that some discomfort might have risen to the surface, and maybe you were tempted to shut the book and call it a day—but if you're still here, good! This is the work we're here to do. It's an opportunity to think, adjust, and truly act on what's important to you.

Meet Lisa. She's a young professional who really wants to be honest and open in her job. She believes in telling the truth, even if it's not the popular thing to do. But at work, it's tough—especially while she's navigating the competitive corporate landscape. For instance, there's a widespread belief in her company, a notorious hedge fund in New York, that employees should always prioritize work over personal life to climb the corporate ladder. While Lisa personally believes in a balanced work–life approach, she often finds herself nodding in agreement during meetings, fearing that expressing her true beliefs might slow her career progression. Sometimes, she goes along with what everyone else is saying, even if it contradicts her beliefs and leaves her drained.

And it doesn't stop there! In team meetings, she keeps her different thoughts to herself. She's constantly worried that people might not like her or her ideas. Online, she aligns her opinions with the trending narratives because she's scared of getting negative comments. So, while Lisa wishes she could always stand by the truth, sometimes she chooses to fit in instead.

Realizing there's a gap between what you want to be and how you act is a big first step. And guess what? It's okay to admit it. After all, you can't make changes if you don't see and *accept* what needs changing.

You can't make changes
if you don't see and *accept*
what needs changing.

In Lisa's case, her embodied value is acceptance. She tends to value being liked or fitting in. And although it's not a negative value altogether, it's working against her. As we explored in Chapter 1, we all want to be accepted and feel part of a group—it's human. But sometimes, this can make you act differently from what you truly believe in.

So, how can Lisa, or any of us, start acting more like the person we want to be? How can we bridge the gap? Let's dive into an exercise that can help.

YOUR VALUES CHECK-IN: BRIDGING THE GAP

Step 1: Reflect and Recognize
- Write down the values you believe in, the ones you'd *like* to live by. Maybe it's "freedom," "loyalty," or "compassion"—whatever speaks to your heart.
- Reflect on the past week. Think about moments when you acted in line with these values and moments when you didn't. Were there times you chose acceptance over honesty? Or peace over truth? Write those down.

Step 2: Identify the Gaps
- Now, with that list, circle the moments when your actions were in tune with your values. Then underline the moments when they weren't.
- Take a good look. What's causing these gaps? Fear? A need to fit in? Recognizing *why* you do certain things can help you figure out how to change.

Step 3: Bridge the Gap
- Think of one way you can act more in line with each value in the coming week. For Lisa, this could be speaking up at a team

---

meeting. For you, maybe it's showing gratitude when you usually stay silent or standing up for fairness when it's easier to stay out of it.

- It's all about small steps. Meet yourself where you are, then go a step further. Each choice you make will bring you closer to being the person you want to be. I mean, your choices are already creating an identity, why not make it a conscious occurrence!

Step 4: Embrace the Journey

- I know that this one can sound like a clichéd step in self-help-speak, but I'll say it anyway: you will *need* to understand that this is a journey. There's no way around it. There will be days when you rock it and days when you slip. Get up and keep going. The aim isn't to be perfect, but to keep moving forward.
- When you stumble, see it as a learning point. Ask yourself: What can this teach me? How can I make a different choice next time?

We're all uniquely human, each of us wired with our own set of values that guides how we see and interact with the world. I keep this in mind constantly and make an effort to remind my clients and audience of it as much as possible. I know how easy it can be to project our values onto others or cave under the pressure of other people's projections. My values help me stay true to my own beliefs while still respecting those of others, even when I'm drawing a line in the sand for myself. Whether you're driven by a desire for "freedom," a need for "harmony," or something completely different, always remember that there's no playbook that fits everyone. That's the beauty of The Third Perspective—you get to *choose* what works for you. I'll say it again: there are always options available to you.

The three pillars I'm laying out in this book encourage you not to box yourself into predefined categories but to look within, to truly become aware of your inner world, recognize what resonates with you, and then take responsibility for your stance, as you've done in this chapter. The real beauty lies in discovering your personal truths and pursuing them, even when it's challenging, even when it means standing alone from the crowd.

Now that you have your principles firmly in your toolkit, we're going to dive into your default communication style. It's crucial to figure out how you naturally express yourself—what's working for you and what's falling flat. This self-awareness is vital. It's about taking further responsibility for not just what you say, but *how* you say it. I will be inviting you to get curious about the *why* behind your words. You will take responsibility for your communication, not just in content but in delivery.

So, let's get ready to peel back another layer and come to terms with how you communicate your values to the world. This is where you start to match your voice with your values, and that's where the magic happens.

Chapter 7

Liberate Your Tongue

Find your voice"—we hear it all the time, right? It's a phrase that's thrown around far too often. But let's be real here, it's not just about finding your voice—it's about remembering and rediscovering its power and then using it in a way that makes a difference. That's why I wrote this book—to get past the clichés and dig into what it really takes to communicate bravely, but most of all, effectively. I don't just want you to be inspired, that's not enough; I want you to be impactful. It's easy to ride the wave of motivation, but what happens when that fades? That's when the real work begins. Knowing your values is one thing; being able to express them effectively is another game entirely. That's what we're tackling in this chapter. This is why you're being greeted with these words as we go deeper into Responsibility. Here you will take charge of your voice so you can use it with intention and purpose. At this stage, you will also give yourself back the power and the patience to communicate on your own terms—without hiding.

Using your voice powerfully isn't just about speaking up; you will need to know how to speak in a way that resonates. And guess what? A lot of it comes down to your communication style—a concept that might seem trivial but is crucial. As we work through these pages, we'll uncover and understand the nuances of how you communicate. It's more than the words you choose; it's the tone, the timing, the context—all the layers that make your voice uniquely yours. By taking responsibility for not only what you say but how you say it, you elevate your ability to connect deeply with yourself and those you come across.

Now I can ask you directly: Have you ever paused to think about how you communicate with the world? As someone who believes that communication is both an art and a science, I find myself constantly reflecting on this aspect. In my work with clients, improving communication usually becomes an area we focus on, even though at the start many don't realize the significant role it plays. I understand this because most people want to be handed a strategy immediately—what do I *say*?, what do I *do*? But as we go deeper, they quickly learn that effective communication is like a dance, a delicate balance of verbal expressions and body language, of *listening* and *responding*.

Think of life like a big, dramatic play. In this play, all of us wear different masks depending on the scene—these masks are like the different ways we communicate in various situations. Sometimes you might put on the peacemaker mask, smoothly handling tough situations. Other times, you might step into the shoes of a leader, taking charge and setting the direction. Then there are those moments when you're more like a detective, dropping subtle clues instead of just blurting things out. Like any good actor, sometimes you nail your part, getting your message across just right. But let's be honest, there are also times when things don't go as planned. That's okay—it happens to everyone. The trick is to understand these different "masks" or communication styles you use.

Why does this matter? Well, these styles can significantly change how you see yourself, how other people see you, and how well you connect with them. Each style is useful in its own way, but knowing the right time to use each one—that's the real skill.

Effective communication
is like a dance, a delicate
balance of verbal expressions
and body language, of
listening and *responding.*

WHY YOUR COMMUNICATION STYLE MATTERS

- **Living Under the Digital Spotlight:** Think of social media as the world's biggest stage. A handful of powerful platforms amplify our voices, so every word can reach corners of the globe in seconds. With such a broad audience, it's crucial to communicate clearly and with compassion to prevent minor missteps from becoming major mishaps.

- **Swift Social Consequences:** Ever noticed how fast news travels online? A single post can change the trajectory of careers overnight. By being in tune with how you come across, you can tread carefully on hot topics, ensuring your intentions aren't lost in translation.

- **Healing, Not Hurting:** The collective sabotage game often feels more like "gotcha!" than genuine accountability. Shifting your communication to be more supportive can pave the way for understanding and growth, rather than just dishing out penalties.

- **Elevating the Conversation:** Yelling might grab attention, but it rarely changes minds. By understanding how you communicate, you're better equipped to turn heated debates into productive discussions.

- **Making Connections in Divided Times:** Our world feels split in half sometimes. But a well-tuned communication style can be a bridge-builder, helping you find common ground even when you disagree.

- **Grow as You Go:** The push for accountability in our culture also underscores a thirst for growth and learning. Sharpening your communication skills isn't just about avoiding missteps— it's a commitment to bettering yourself and the world around you.

- **The Power of Pause:** Empathy isn't just a buzzword—it's an essential tool for understanding. In a world that often leaps before it looks, taking a moment to communicate with care and empathy can turn the tide of a conversation.

IDENTIFYING YOUR PRIMARY COMMUNICATION STYLE

Now that you've had a glimpse of the benefits of refining how you communicate, are you ready for a little backstage introspection with our next exercise? (Hint: Your score from the Self-Silencing Scale in Chapter 5 might just be the spotlight you need.)

WHICH COMMUNICATOR ARE YOU?

This exercise is your backstage pass into the world of self-awareness. While we all have our moments of being the diplomat or the leader, there's usually one style we default to, our go-to "communication costume." This isn't about boxing yourself into one category forever, but rather understanding your natural inclinations. By paying close attention to your dominant style, you can better decide whether it's amplifying your voice in the right way or limiting your interactions—which we absolutely do not want!

- **Be Honest:** It's essential to approach this exercise with an open heart and mind. Remember, this is about pinpointing your primary style, not every style you can exhibit.
- **Reflect on Moments:** For each communication style that follows, think back to recent personal or professional experiences that resonate with the given description. Jot down specific incidents.
- **Ask Self-Assessment Questions:** After reading each description, answer the accompanying questions to gauge the frequency with which you embody that style.

- **Connect the Dots:** Lastly, consider your score from the Self-Silencing Scale we discussed in Chapter 5. Does it align with your identified communication style? If there's a mismatch, ponder over it. Why might that be?

Harmonizing Communicator

Description: Often the peacekeeper, valuing agreement and unity even at the cost of personal opinions.

Strengths: You thrive in situations where everyone is on the same page. You can be the glue that holds a group together, making sure that everyone feels heard and included. When things get heated, you're good at cooling things down, although you'd rather not have to deal with conflict to begin with.

Weaknesses: The mask of constant agreeability and trying to keep the peace can become a heavy burden. Over time, by prioritizing others' feelings over your own, you might sometimes forget about your own needs. This could make you feel left out or even resentful. Constantly being the peacekeeper might lead you to keep your true feelings bottled up.

Reflect: Can you recall a situation when you suppressed your views to maintain harmony?

Questions:
- How often do you compromise your views to avoid confrontation?
  (Always) (Often) (Sometimes) (Rarely) (Never)
- Do you feel drained or frustrated after constantly agreeing?
  (Always) (Often) (Sometimes) (Rarely) (Never)

Assertive-Plus Communicator

Description: The confident voice in the room, leading discussions, and sometimes overshadowing others.

Strengths: Your confidence is infectious. You bring energy and direction to a group, making sure that decisions are made and actions are taken. With you taking the lead, projects get done and people feel inspired.

Weaknesses: But, sometimes, you can come on too strong. Being the main voice all the time can overshadow others. This means you might miss out on great ideas from those who speak less. Your bold style might make others hold back their thoughts, creating a space where only the boldest opinions shine through.

Reflect: Think of the last time you dominated a conversation. How did others respond?

Questions:
- How frequently do you find yourself leading discussions or brainstorming sessions?
    (Always) (Often) (Sometimes) (Rarely) (Never)
- Do you often sense that your strong opinions might stifle others?
    (Always) (Often) (Sometimes) (Rarely) (Never)

Indirect Communicator

Description: Subtle in expression, often using nuanced phrases that mask true feelings.

Strengths: There are times when being blunt might not be the best approach, and that's when your subtle way of expressing things comes in handy. You have a knack for sharing your thoughts without sparking open conflict.

Weaknesses: On the flip side, always leaning into these subtle hints can make you shy away from speaking up plainly. Others might find themselves constantly trying to decipher what you truly mean. It can become a game of reading between the lines. This indirect approach can sometimes lead to confusion or people getting the wrong idea, which can even heighten tensions unintentionally.

Reflect: Remember a time when you gave feedback indirectly. Was your intention understood?

Questions:
- How often do you find yourself using subtleties rather than being straightforward?
     (Always) (Often) (Sometimes) (Rarely) (Never)
- Do you worry that being direct might lead to confrontation?
     (Always) (Often) (Sometimes) (Rarely) (Never)

Assertive Communicator
Description: Balanced in communication, respecting both your own feelings and those of others.

Strengths: You have a gift for straightforward, clear communication. When you speak, people listen and feel appreciated. Your approach makes others feel understood, building a bridge of trust and open conversation.

Weaknesses: But be careful—being direct can sometimes be mistaken for being pushy or too intense. It's essential to check in with yourself and ensure your assertiveness doesn't unintentionally edge into being overpowering or disregarding of others.

Reflect: Recall a situation when you communicated an issue clearly without being aggressive.

Questions:
- How frequently do you ensure both your perspective and that of the other person are respected in conversations?
  (Always) (Often) (Sometimes) (Rarely) (Never)
- Do you feel you strike a balance between listening and expressing?
  (Always) (Often) (Sometimes) (Rarely) (Never)

After going through these questions, take a moment to tally up your responses. If you notice a trend of "Always" and "Often" answers leaning toward a particular style, that's probably your primary mode of communication. Now that you've got this snapshot of your communication persona, let's talk about why this matters so much.

In this rapidly changing world, brave communication isn't just a neat skill to have, it's a necessity. Whether it's standing up in a meeting, voicing a concern with a friend, or advocating for a cause you believe in, the way you communicate plays a huge role in the impact you make. And this is something I wholeheartedly stand by.

Let me give you an example. At a leading medical research company, Thomas was known as "the bulldozer." Everyone knew not to cross his path during debates. You might have come across the type. I sure have. During a key team meeting, a colleague, Dr. Reina, started to share new data showing that a widely used drug might cause serious side effects for certain ethnic groups. Before she could finish, Thomas, who had full faith in the history of the drug, slammed his hand on the table and dismissed her: "This drug has been around for years! Stop trying to create problems where there are none!"

Dr. Reina, who was holding valuable data that could save lives, felt humiliated, intimidated, and silenced. As a result, she hesitated to push her findings further. Six months later, national news highlighted the very side effects Dr. Reina had discovered, and lawsuits flooded in. Thomas's unchecked aggression had not just cost the company its reputation, but had endangered lives.

After witnessing the weighty cost of her silence, Dr. Reina came across my work online and felt an immediate resonance. Like many people, she'd never heard the term "self-censorship" before, but after listening to me break it down in great detail, she realized that it was something she'd been doing for most of her life. Accepting that something needed to change, and fast, she reached out and, over the next year, we worked very closely together. Like you and I are about to do, one of the first things we did was explore whether her communication style (in this case, harmonizing) was serving her best interests or holding her back. You can probably guess what the answer was.

You see, understanding your default style is like having a road map of your mind. When you're unaware of how you *naturally* present yourself, you might find yourself getting lost, *misunderstood*, or even steamrolled in conversations. But by identifying your go-to style, you arm yourself with awareness. It's like turning on a light in a previously dim room. Suddenly, you can see the furniture, the walls, and the path forward.

Imagine trying to change the direction of a boat without knowing which way it's currently heading. That's the equivalent of attempting to communicate bravely without understanding your inherent style. By coming to terms with your natural tendencies, you can steer your communication ship with purpose and direction, ensuring that you're heard, understood, and respected.

When you're unaware of how you *naturally* present yourself, you might find yourself getting lost, *misunderstood*, or even steamrolled in conversations.

As you step out in your personal and professional life, taking responsibility for your communication style will be a game changer. This seemingly simple exercise tends to be one of the biggest "aha" moments for each person I work with. I regularly revisit this practice myself, at least twice a year, to reflect on any shifts in how I communicate. For instance, I've noticed that while I typically adopt an assertive style in work and with friends and family, in romantic relationships, a passive-aggressive side can surface when I feel cornered or misunderstood. This realization wasn't just insightful; it was a call to take responsibility for how I communicate in *all* aspects of my life.

Keep in mind, this is not about changing the essence of who you are. It's more about taking accountability, owning up to how you communicate, and polishing the way you put your thoughts and feelings out there. By understanding your communication style, you're laying the groundwork for more genuine and powerful conversations in your day-to-day life. We all have our default ways of communicating, but it's interesting how we might switch it up depending on who we're talking to. Recognizing these patterns and being able to put a name to them will help you in the long term. It allows you to spot when you might be veering off course and helps you steer back to where you want to be.

So, take this knowledge and use it to your advantage. After all, in a world full of noise, your voice matters, and it deserves to be heard in its truest form. What you are doing here is getting closer to embodying the philosophy of The Third Perspective. You are, once again, finding the balance between staying rooted in the most honest parts of yourself while remaining open to adapting to different situations.

REFINING YOUR COMMUNICATION STYLE

You've already done a lot of work in this chapter, and I have to take a moment to commend you for that. In writing this book I didn't just want you to finish with some more theory in your mind. I wanted to make sure I gave you self-reflective tools to help you create a road map that is unique to you. I know that this level of introspection is not natural or always comfortable for people, myself included. It has to be a conscious practice, one cemented by actual effort and an integration of what you learn. Instead of waiting for motivation and inspiration to strike, repeated effort will keep you going. Don't get me wrong, motivation is lovely, but it's not reliable. Small, repeated efforts are. And if you're still with me and engaging thoughtfully with these exercises, that's exactly what you're doing, and it's admirable.

Now, let's see what tangible changes we can make. The reflective exercise you completed previously gave you a clearer picture of your primary communication style. It's time to put this new understanding into practice—to actively shape how you interact with the world around you:

- **Watch Yourself Talk:** Start by closely watching your own communication patterns in different settings. Are you the peacemaker in family discussions, the assertive voice that leads in work meetings, or the indirect communicator in romantic relationships? Keep an eye on these habits and think about whether they match up with the way you see your own communication style.
- **Make Small Adjustments:** Now that you've noticed how you communicate, try tweaking things a little. Those small adjustments will add up. For example, if you usually hint around instead of saying what you mean, try being more straight-to-the-point. Express yourself directly. Or, if you're often the one leading the conversation, try taking a step back to let others share their thoughts. See what changes when you give others a chance to speak up.

- **Feedback Seeking:** Actively reach out to your friends, family, or coworkers and ask what they think about the way you communicate. Getting their point of view can really open your eyes and help you understand how others see and experience your communication style. This is an example of when outside perspectives can be enlightening. You might be tempted to skip this step (I can see you!) because it brings forth a lot of vulnerability, but this is exactly why you need to follow through.

- **Listen Like a Pro:** Regardless of how you usually communicate, learning the skill of active listening is invaluable. Focus on paying close attention to how others are communicating, both with their words and their body language, and give thoughtful responses. We'll dive into the specifics of listening in the next chapter.

- **Role-Playing Scenarios:** I often recommend role-playing to my clients because it works. If you can, do some role-playing exercises with someone you trust. It's a great way to practice different ways of talking and reacting in a relaxed, low-stakes, no-pressure setting. Plus, it can be quite fun if you get into it.

- **Reflection Journaling:** Keep a journal to document and reflect on the different experiences you have when you talk to people. You'll record the times that went well and those that didn't. And think about how you felt and reacted. This practice is effective for tracking your progress and, most importantly, identifying areas you can work on. Emphasis on *work*.

- **Become a Student:** No matter where you are in life, you're not above learning from others. Consider working with a mentor or enrolling in workshops or courses focused on communication skills. These can give you specific advice and help based on *how* you talk and what you want to get better at.

- **Mindful Moments:** Practicing mindfulness or meditation can really boost your self-awareness, especially when you're talking to others. These methods can help you notice the ways you usually communicate and what sets off your emotions.

By embracing and getting into these practices, which I can't recommend enough, you're doing much more than understanding your communication style; you're actively refining and evolving it. Most people will never get to do that in their lifetime, at least not consciously—but you can! You already *are*. The work you're doing is deeply connected to the core principles of The Third Perspective—looking inward and taking accountability in your interactions with others. To truly push back on the level of intolerance that surrounds us today, we, as individuals, have to be willing to create an environment of thoughtfulness within ourselves. This ensures that your communication is not only effective, but also a genuine reflection and representation of who you are.

Now that you've established a solid understanding of your verbal communication, it's important to turn your attention to a crucial yet frequently underestimated aspect of interacting with others: good ol' body language.

BEYOND VERBAL EXPRESSION

Think of body language as the *silent* yet impactful partner to your words. Every day, as you interact with the world around you, you're saying a lot without speaking a word. The way you move your hands, the tilt of your head, the raise of an eyebrow, the tone of your voice, even the very rhythm of your breathing—they all send messages, sometimes more powerful than words themselves. It's like our bodies have their own way of talking without words, sharing feelings and thoughts, especially when words just don't do the trick.

Think of body language
as the *silent* yet impactful
partner to your words.

When I speak to people about undoing self-censorship, I always make it very clear that we put way too much pressure on what we should say with the spoken word, but I think when you bring the focus onto "Who am I *being* in each interaction?" without overly analyzing, pathologizing, or being obsessive about it, it can be a very exciting exploration. If you start to become a little more curious about the messages you are sending without uttering a single word, what more could you learn about yourself and how the world responds to you?

Imagine two old friends catching up in a coffee shop after being apart for years. One shares a tough time they went through. They might sound strong when they talk about it, but the little things, like a shaky hand or a quick look down, show they're still hurting. Seeing this, their friend might just give their hand a squeeze. That simple gesture says, "I'm here for you," without them needing to say anything.

Or a corporate boardroom where a stakeholder is pitching a significant proposal. Sure, they have a great script talking about all the good points of the project. But what really sells it? It's the way they look everyone in the eye, keep their palms open as if saying, "I've got nothing to hide," and speak in a voice that's both strong and welcoming. That's what shows everyone they really believe in what they're pitching.

Even in simple everyday moments, this silent language plays out. Picture yourself on a crowded train: You see a younger person giving up their seat for someone older than them. They might not say anything, but the older person's nod and small smile say "thank you" loud and clear. In return, the younger person's quiet smile shows they're happy to help and respect the gesture. It's all in the little looks and gestures.

Sometimes, what people say and how they act don't match up, and it feels "off." Imagine someone saying "congrats" on a big win, but they're not really smiling, or they're looking away, or their voice sounds fake-happy. Even if you don't spot exactly what's wrong, you can tell they might not mean it. It just shows how powerful body language and tone can be. You might be verbally expressing agreement, but if your arms are crossed and your gaze averted, your body could be signaling the opposite. This nonverbal aspect of communication is a key component of The Third Perspective—our focus is to go beyond what is said, and tap into how it is expressed in a holistic sense. It's worth remembering that all of this isn't about decoding the body language of others, *although you'll be able to do that too*, which is a fantastic bonus. The goal is getting to know and use your own unspoken signals.

DIGITAL BODY LANGUAGE

Your body is like a live storybook, showing how you feel inside. Little facial expressions, the way you talk, how you stand, and many other small signs say a lot about you. Let's step back into the world of social media for a moment, a place where your words are your primary tool, but even here, the way you use them can convey body language–like signals. For instance, the use of emojis, punctuation, and even the rhythm of your writing can mirror nonverbal cues in a face-to-face conversation. Consider how a carefully placed smiley face can soften a message or how using ALL CAPS can convey intensity or enthusiasm, much like a raised voice or animated gestures would in person.

Additionally, the timing of your responses on social media, the kind of content you choose to share or interact with, and even the format of your posts can reflect aspects of your "digital body language." A prompt and thoughtful reply might show attentiveness, much like maintaining eye contact in a physical conversation. A well-curated feed can reflect aspects of your personality just as your attire and posture might do in a physical setting. These are things that many of us don't consider, and I'd love for you to bring this awareness to the forefront when you walk back into your digital spaces.

This awareness and alignment of your digital expression with your genuine self are elements of our work together that shouldn't be skipped. It encourages a full-spectrum approach to communication, where every word, pause, and symbol plays an important role in putting forward your message and connecting you with others. This isn't just fluff—these things really matter in how you come across and connect with others, whether you're having an exchange on social media or speaking to someone face-to-face. By being conscious of these elements, you gift yourself with a better chance of getting the results you want in your interactions, both online and offline. Although no outcome is promised, the chances of satisfaction are higher!

YOUR BODY LANGUAGE TAKEAWAYS: ONLINE AND OFFLINE

Digital Presence Across Platforms

Why It Matters: As more interactions shift online, the way you present yourself in virtual settings becomes important. From live streams on social media to webinars, the nonverbal cues we've explored are key to making a strong impression. Whether you're leading the conversation or participating as an audience member, your body language on-screen speaks volumes about your engagement, professionalism, and confidence.

What to Do: Be mindful of how you come across on various digital platforms. When you're live streaming or creating social media videos, let your personality shine through. Use expressive facial expressions and gestures to connect with your audience. Show them your excitement and engagement. In more formal settings like webinars or professional video meetings, keep an alert and upright posture. Nod to show you're following along and use facial expressions that demonstrate you're actively listening and involved. Remember, your presence on-screen, even when you're not speaking, is a constant form of communication (see the following box for more tips on this). Stand out as a brave communicator by the way you carry yourself in these digital interactions.

ADAPTING TO DIFFERENT VIDEO CONTEXTS

The digital era demands versatility in how we present ourselves, especially in video formats. I'm adding some extra points here on video because it is one of the places where we tend to shrink our expression because we're afraid of looking silly in some way. Different online video settings call for varied approaches to body language. Can you see now why courageous expression goes beyond what you say? A relaxed and conversational body language suits social media live videos, while formal and structured nonverbal communication is ideal for professional settings like webinars or business meetings. Recognizing and adapting to these nuances is essential for effective digital communication.

Adjust your body language based on the type of video interaction you're engaging in. In informal settings like live streams or casual social media videos, feel free to adopt a more relaxed posture and use natural, spontaneous gestures to connect with your audience. If you watch any of my live streams on social media, you will notice that I'm much more relaxed in my body language, and I'll probably be brewing a pot of tea while I'm speaking to my audience. In contrast, for formal settings like webinars or business meetings, you can opt for a more professional demeanor. Practice controlled gestures, maintain a steady and focused gaze, and make sure that your posture exudes confidence and attentiveness. This deliberate adaptability in your nonverbal communication will help you project the appropriate image and meet the expectations of your audience, whether you're casually connecting or conducting serious business discussions.

Mastering Eye Contact

Why It Matters: Eye contact is a cornerstone of nonverbal communication. It's a direct way to convey emotions and intentions, helping to establish trust and show engagement in face-to-face interactions. I'm aware that this can differ from culture to culture, but generally speaking, mastering eye contact is vital for creating a connection and demonstrating your attention and respect to the speaker.

What to Do: As you engage in conversations, I encourage you to practice maintaining balanced eye contact. This doesn't mean a continuous, unblinking stare until a single tear falls from your eye, but rather an attentive gaze that communicates your focus and interest. If direct eye contact feels too intense, relax and focus on the area around the person's eyes. It's a less intense way to maintain a connection without the discomfort of direct staring. Remember to take natural breaks in eye contact—doing so makes the interaction feel more relaxed and less intimidating. Aim to reconnect frequently after these breaks, ensuring the other person feels acknowledged and heard. Striking the right balance in eye contact is key: too little can seem disengaged or distant, while too much may come across as overly intense. With practice, you'll find the sweet spot where your eye contact enhances communication for you.

Tonal Touch

Why It Matters: Your voice's tone, pitch, and volume are powerful elements of communication. They add depth and emotion to your words, greatly influencing how your message is received. The right tone makes your words more impactful, helping you connect better with others.

What to Do: I encourage you to consciously practice varying your voice's tone and volume to fit the situation you're in. When discussing serious or important matters, use a strong and clear voice to present authority and confidence. When sharing personal stories or more sensitive topics, use a softer, gentler tone to create an atmosphere of intimacy and trust. By shifting your vocal tone, you can enhance the emotional impact of your message, making your communication more effective and engaging.

The Power of Posture

Why It Matters: Your body tells a story even before you start speaking. It's a nonverbal cue that expresses confidence, openness, and attentiveness. A good posture not only influences how others perceive you, but also affects your own mindset and level of engagement in the conversation.

What to Do: When standing, maintain a posture with a straight back and feet hip-width apart, as this stance exudes confidence and stability. In seated conversations, avoid slouching. Instead, lean forward slightly to indicate active engagement. This subtle shift in posture can dramatically alter how engaged and present you appear in a conversation. One of my favorite things to do when I'm sitting in conversation with someone is bringing the awareness to my body and making small adjustments so I can communicate openness. This also does the job of keeping me calm and centered.

Reading Facial Expressions

Why It Matters: Facial expressions are the silent narrators of your emotional state. If there's one thing you take from this section, let it be this! They provide context to your words and can significantly enhance the effectiveness of your communication.

What to Do: Pay attention to your facial reactions. Try practicing in front of a mirror to understand how different expressions alter the perception of what you're saying. Think of your face like a book cover—it gives a sneak peek into what you're feeling inside. A genuine smile can make someone feel good and reassured, and lifting your eyebrows can show you're surprised or asking a question. Being aware of your facial expressions allows you to align them more effectively with your spoken words.

Breathing with Purpose

Why It Matters: Controlled breathing is not just for relaxation; it's a vital tool for clear and calm communication. It helps regulate your speech and ensures that your nerves don't get the better of you during important and potentially difficult conversations or interactions.

What to Do: Integrate deliberate deep breathing into your conversations. This technique helps you to pace your words so you can speak from a place of clarity and maintain calmness. It's another personal go-to. Practice makes perfect with controlled breathing—the more you do it, the more natural it will become.

Using Your Space

Why It Matters: The way you move and occupy space during a conversation can add emphasis to your message and help in putting your emotions forward more effectively.

What to Do: Use hand gestures to emphasize key points. Be mindful of how your movements can enhance or distract from your message. Stepping closer or moving away can dynamically alter the intensity of your communication. For example, placing a hand on someone's shoulder can be a show of empathy and comfort, while stepping forward during a presentation can underscore an important point. Think of your physical movements as an integral component of your communication style.

The aim with all the work we're doing isn't to craft a perfect, theatrical performance every time you communicate. You don't have to put on a show every time you talk. All you're doing is remembering that your movement has an impact on your conviction and people wanting to listen to you and your views and opinions. Whether I'm having a private conversation with one of my siblings, onstage speaking to hundreds of people, doing a live stream for my audience, or sitting around the dinner table with a group of friends, I pay attention to my body, and I involve it in my speech. You can make this alignment a practice, too.

This alignment does more than just help you get your point across—it boosts your confidence. It has a positive impact on how you carry yourself. I can feel the difference in my body when there's a disconnect between my words and bodily actions. By making sure that every part of you resonates with what you're saying, you're less likely to doubt yourself or hold back. Going forward, I want you to think of yourself as a musical instrument, where every part needs to be in harmony to produce the most beautiful sound. In the same way, when every aspect of you works together, your message becomes something that deeply resonates with others. But, most of all, it will resonate with *you*.

Your next step? Pay attention. Notice how you and others use body language. Watch for the stories told without words. As you become more aware, work on using your gestures, tone, and delivery to share your message better. Remember, every move you make and every pause can help show what you truly feel and believe.

Before we come to the end of this chapter, I want to ground these ideas into a real-life scenario by asking you to imagine you're in the midst of a heated online group discussion. Opinions are clashing and the conversation is teetering on the edge of hostility. As you pause, fingers poised over the keyboard, your body language, as you now know, is worth paying attention to in this moment. Your posture, the tension in your shoulders, even the depth of your breath, all reflect and impact the emotional tone of your message. You're suddenly hyperaware of how your next words could either fuel the fire or redirect the conversation to calmer waters. Or at least you hope so!

This heightened awareness of your body's responses is not just an exercise in self-awareness, but a vital part of effective communication. It's about bridging that gap between your physical presence and your digital expression. As you sit there, considering your next move, your body language can either escalate your stress, narrowing your perspective, or it can help you find a calmer, more centered place from which to respond.

This is where the understanding of your communication style becomes instrumental. You're not only taking steps to break the cycle of self-censorship; you're refining your social filter if you've previously been reckless with your words. Your choice of words online, influenced by your communication style, carries weight. If your style is assertive, your response might naturally be direct and clear, cutting through the noise. Or you might choose that this is not a hill worth dying on and allow for your grounded silence to speak volumes. If you lean toward a more harmonizing style, you might look for ways to defuse the tension. But, regardless of your style, being mindful of your physical state can help you choose words that are not just reactive but reflective of your true intent.

I wanted to offer you this scenario because it perfectly captures what we've been exploring together. You've got insights and a handle on your communication style *and* you're getting the hang of using body language to your advantage. This is huge. These aren't just fancy concepts; they're practical tools that can help you deal with tricky situations with a mix of responsibility and empathy. You have once again tapped into the magic that lies at the core of The Third Perspective—a place where you balance your internal state with your external expression, making sure that your communication, in every form, *truly* reflects your core values and worldview.

In the next chapter, we'll delve into the art of listening. You're going to discover your listening style and learn how to meld it with your supportive communication style. It goes beyond hearing words; you will understand contexts, emotions, and unspoken messages. In a world where everyone seems to be shouting to be heard, the power of listening can't be overstated. It's transformative, not just in public discussions, but in our personal relationships too. I know I'll be revisiting this advice next time I find myself in a disagreement with a loved one.

So, as we move forward, I invite you to pause, maybe grab yourself a glass of water, and prepare for what's to come. Whether you choose to continue now or return with a fresh and more open perspective tomorrow, the key is to keep engaging with the material. Do not pull the plug on yourself and your progress. The next chapter might just revolutionize the way you think about what it means to not only listen, but to listen *well*.

Chapter 8

Be Quick to Listen, Slow to Speak

In a world where opinions are fired off at lightning speed and being right often trumps being open, truly listening has become a rare superpower. The Greek philosopher Epictetus said, "We have two ears and one mouth so that we can listen twice as much as we speak." This wisdom resonates deeply, especially now. While much of our focus is on how to articulate our thoughts, the equally important art of listening tends to be overshadowed. To truly connect, discover deep insights, and courageously wade through our complex times, marrying your speech with genuine, attentive listening is essential. This is particularly vital in your journey of taking responsibility and undoing self-censorship because listening opens you up to a broader range of ideas and perspectives. If you welcome those perspectives through a critical, yet open, lens, it'll enrich your understanding and aid in breaking you free from the confines of limited thinking. Sounds good to me!

I'll admit, I wasn't always great at this. When I look back on past conflicts and relationships, I realize I often only heard what I wanted to, missing out on the full picture. I'd cherry-pick parts of a conversation to suit my own motivations. And there would be many times when I would "hear" something that was never said. Times when I'd activated selective hearing and ended up being dismissive toward a partner, a friend, or a family member. I've learned that real listening is more than being silent while the other person is talking. You have to truly hear them, instead of just waiting for your turn to speak. You have to accept that you don't have all the answers. You have to find courage in admitting, "I was wrong," or asking, "Can you tell me more?"

In our fast-paced, react-first world, mastering listening is so much more than adding another skill to your arsenal; it's a form of intellectual humility. This humility acknowledges the limits of your knowledge and recognizes that every voice, even those you disagree with, can have something valuable to offer. We each have our unique way of listening. And while we might switch between styles, most of us have a go-to mode, our "default listening channel." Understanding this default, exactly as you did with your communication, will cause a welcome shift in all of your interactions.

IDENTIFYING YOUR GO-TO LISTENING STYLE

Let's now focus on tuning into your "listening radio" and identifying its primary frequency. The upcoming exercise is designed to be your guide through the diverse world of listening styles. By the end, you'll have a clearer picture of your listening strengths and areas for growth.

So, are you ready to discover which listener you are?

WHICH LISTENER ARE YOU?

Think of this exercise as tuning into your favorite radio station. We all have our go-to channel when it comes to listening, that one style we naturally lean into most often. By spotting which channel you're usually tuned into, you can better understand and connect with yourself and others. You won't be pigeonholing yourself into a category; you'll be fine-tuning your listening so you can capture the *full* melody of every conversation.

- **Open Ears:** Approach this exercise introspectively. We're focusing on identifying your primary listening mode, not every mode you might tap into occasionally. Do not judge anything you discover, simply collect information.

- **Flashback Moments:** For each listening style described, think of a recent moment when you felt most aligned with that description. Write down the specifics of that memory.
- **Self-Reflection Questions:** After each description, take some time to think about the given questions and see how often you resort to that style.
- **The Sound of Silence:** Now think about whether your primary communication style, as determined in the previous chapter, matches with your listening style. Are they in harmony or is there a disconnect? Let's find out.

Analytical Listener

Description: You focus on details, facts, and logic; you're keen on getting to the crux of the matter.

Strengths: Precision is your forte. When someone shares, you catch the nuances and specifics. You're great at dissecting complex problems and challenging oversimplifications—which makes you the one to turn to when clarity is required.

Weaknesses: At times, you might miss out on the emotional nuances or the broader message as you delve deep into specifics.

Reflect: Think of a discussion where you zoned in on specific data or facts. Did it help or hinder the conversation?

Questions:
- How often do you seek detailed explanations or specifics in discussions?
  (Always) (Often) (Sometimes) (Rarely) (Never)

153

- Do you sometimes feel restless when details are skipped?
     (Always) (Often) (Sometimes) (Rarely) (Never)

Global Listener

Description: You see the forest, not just the trees. You're good at zooming out and this is where your attention naturally goes.

Strengths: Your broad perspective often helps in understanding the purpose or the "why" behind conversations. You can rise above the gritty details and appreciate the broader context of opposing views.

Weaknesses: In your quest for the big picture, smaller and critical details might sometimes elude you. You might also find yourself holding back from being specific and saying what you really want to say because it feels safer to zoom out.

Reflect: Can you remember a conversation where you got the central theme but missed out on some specifics?

Questions:
- How often do you focus on the central message over individual data points or specific details?
     (Always) (Often) (Sometimes) (Rarely) (Never)
- Do you find detailed discussions a bit tedious?
     (Always) (Often) (Sometimes) (Rarely) (Never)

Relational Listener

Description: You are attuned to the emotional pulse of the conversation, sensing and often reflecting the speaker's emotions. You might consider yourself an empath.

Strengths: You create a safe space for sharing, as people feel genuinely heard and understood around you. In contentious discussions, you can bring a much-needed sense of compassion and empathy.

Weaknesses: At times, you might become so enveloped in the emotional aspect that you miss out on the factual content.

Reflect: Remember an instance when you deeply resonated with someone's emotions during a conversation. How did it affect the discussion's outcome?

Questions:
- How often do you find yourself mirroring the emotions of the speaker?

   (Always) (Often) (Sometimes) (Rarely) (Never)
- Do you prioritize understanding feelings over facts in conversations?

   (Always) (Often) (Sometimes) (Rarely) (Never)

Task-Oriented Listener
Description: You're focused on solutions, actions, and results. You're keen on identifying the problem and fixing it.

Strengths: Your pragmatism ensures that discussions are efficient and to-the-point. You can steer conversations toward constructive outcomes rather than heated disputes.

Weaknesses: Your solution-oriented approach might make you jump to conclusions before understanding the entire scenario. Sometimes impatience gets in the way of you staying present, which can lead to cutting people off prematurely.

Reflect: Can you think of a time when you offered a solution before fully understanding the issue?

Questions:

- How frequently do you catch yourself giving solutions or advice in discussions?

    (Always) (Often) (Sometimes) (Rarely) (Never)

- Do you sometimes feel impatient when conversations aren't direct or solution-focused?

    (Always) (Often) (Sometimes) (Rarely) (Never)

Post-Assessment: Take a moment to review your responses. If a pattern emerges with "Always" and "Often" leaning toward one style, it's likely your dominant listening mode. Remember, the key is not to box yourself, but to understand and refine.

REFINING YOUR LISTENING STYLE

When you figure out how you usually listen, it's like finding your groove. You'll see what you're great at and areas where you might need a bit more practice. Remember that the dance of communication isn't led by the speakers alone. Listeners, too, carry the rhythm forward. Own your listening style, understand it, and refine it as needed. "In a world of talkers, be a listener."

If you're a talker, you'll naturally struggle with letting others "run" the discussion. This is normal as you readjust and rewire. But listening doesn't mean you go without social power. The right question or remark after a long silence is equally impactful. Today, we are all too eager to voice our opinions, quick to defend our beliefs, and even quicker to dismiss or deride those who differ. It's become far too easy to shut out those we don't agree with, to isolate ourselves within echo chambers of like-mindedness, and it's making us miserable and unable

The dance of
communication isn't led
by the speakers alone.
Listeners, too, carry
the rhythm forward.

to have interesting and insightful conversations. But I don't believe that's the way it needs to be forever. I'm convinced that this isn't a permanent state. By understanding your listening style, you can make conversations more fluid and avoid unnecessary misunderstandings. It helps you see that behind every viewpoint is a real person with their own story. Get curious about how they arrived at their thinking. Agreeing isn't always the goal; sometimes, it's more about seeing where the other person is coming from. It's your way of showing that you hear them and are open to considering their perspective without immediate negative judgment.

And here's the secret tool in all of this: emotional intelligence (also known as EQ). To truly master effective communication, you will need this. When you develop your EQ, you're enhancing your ability to listen and understand others. You don't just hear words; you practice sensing the emotions and intentions behind them. This skill, which you likely have but just need to give it a workout, will help you approach conversations with sensitivity and awareness. With a heightened EQ, you'll be more in tune with the subtleties of dialogue. You'll pick up on those nonverbal cues, sense underlying feelings, and respond in ways that are both thoughtful and considerate. You won't only be avoiding misunderstandings; you'll be building bridges along the way.

THE "OPEN EARS, OPEN HEART" CONVERSATION

Consider this exercise, yet another personal favorite, as a crucial work-out for your speaking and listening skills. This is where we bring both aspects together into a single, harmonious practice. You're going to practice talking and paying attention in a way that makes people feel heard and understood. Even if you think you're already good at doing this, there's always room for improvement. Focusing solely on how polarized the world is is futile if we are not willing to examine the way we are interacting with others. Right now, in real time. This is where The Third Perspective comes back into full focus. You are here to find common ground instead of feeding into the division, both of which can happen in the micro-interactions you have with people. And you get to choose which side you will feed. This approach ties directly into the responsibility you have to communicate effectively and empathetically. Shall we?

- **Select a Partner:** Choose a friend, family member, or colleague for this exercise. Ideally, pick someone you trust and with whom you'd like to enhance your communication.

- **Choose a Topic:** Pick a subject that you have differing opinions on. It doesn't have to be a controversial topic; it can be something as simple as a movie preference or as complex as a philosophical belief.

- **Set Some Ground Rules:** Before you start, agree on a few ground rules. Each person gets an *uninterrupted* time to speak. Key word here: *uninterrupted*. The listener's role is to focus entirely on understanding the speaker's viewpoint, not to come up with a response right away.

- **Pick a Speaker Role:** As the speaker, express your views on the topic. Remember, the goal isn't to convince the other person, but to explain your thinking and the reasons behind it clearly.

- **Pick a Listener Role:** As the listener, your job is to listen actively. This means giving the speaker your full attention, not cutting them off or preparing a counterargument in your head. Your main aim is to understand the speaker's feelings and where they are coming from. After they're done talking, repeat back what you heard, but in your own words. You'll do this to make sure you're on the same page. Even if you don't agree, you can show them you get it: "So, if I'm hearing correctly, you're saying you feel like this because…"

- **Switch Roles:** Once the first round is complete, switch roles. The speaker becomes the listener and vice versa.
- **Reflect Together:** After both rounds, take a few minutes to discuss the experience. How did it feel to speak without being interrupted? How was it to listen without immediately jumping into defense mode?
- **Reflect Personally:** After the conversation, take some time to think about how it went. Write down what you noticed about how you speak. Were there moments when you struggled to listen without interrupting? Be honest. Did showing you understood what they were saying change how the conversation went?

If you've made it this far, I want to challenge you: bookmark this exercise and make a plan to actually do it, not just read about it. This is an important step—taking what you've learned off the page and into real life. I truly find this exercise to be a game changer. It moves you from just "listening to respond" to "listening to understand"—and whether you realize it or not, all that's been revealed to you plays a significant role in the shape your voice takes. It all has a direct impact on what you say and what you choose to keep to yourself. Instead of just waiting for our turn to talk, you're trying to "get" what the other person's saying. By focusing on understanding and showing them that you get their point of view, your conversations become more collaborative and less confrontational. Keep at it, and you might just find your conversations getting better and better. Who knows, maybe even pleasurable!

And this is a great lead-in to our next chapter on self-reputation. Here, you'll learn how important it is to accept that being misunderstood is the name of the game if you're going to be doing *anything* brave in life. You'll discover how to build a solid reputation with yourself, so you don't have to rely on *others* to validate your feelings and opinions. This is all about having the confidence to express your-self in the face of potential criticism or possible cancellation, and it ties right back to the work you've just done on understanding and communicating. So, as you keep practicing those listening and speak-ing skills, remember that they're laying the groundwork for a stronger, more resilient you.

It's time to explore how building a resilient self-reputation can revolutionize your conversations, including your entire approach to communication and existing in the world as a human being who chooses to live boldly both in the world and behind closed doors.

Chapter 9

Honest Conflict or
Dishonest Harmony?

Your reputation is your responsibility, not something others hand to you. It's built in those quiet moments when you choose to do the right thing, even when it's tough, not when you're looking for applause or trying to dodge criticism. In a world where we're lured into chasing "likes" and approval, the reputation that stands the test of time is the one you create for yourself. It's when you're firm in who you are, without being swayed by every passing trend or opinion. It's when you know that your true worth comes from your character, not what others say about you. The work we're doing together requires you to build a self-reputation that's so strong and true, it doesn't waver, no matter how much public opinion changes. Within The Third Perspective framework, crafting a resilient self-reputation is a key act of personal responsibility. That's why we're talking about it here, in connection with the insights on speaking and listening we've explored. It involves being mindful of how your actions align with your core values and your beliefs. It's about taking responsibility for distinguishing constructive criticism from mere noise and using it to become more grounded in who you are. It's where you recognize that you are, and have always been, the *architect* of your own image.

In this chapter, my aim is to show you that external reputation is fickle. It indicates something and, by all means, you should to a degree

You are, and have always
been, the *architect* of
your own image.

care what people think about you, otherwise you will find it very difficult to maintain intimacy with the world around you. But relying on it? That's a whole different story. The reputation you have "out there" can vanish in a gust of the latest trend. When the storm hits, will you have your back? That's what I care about most, and you should too. Will you, even when trembling, doubting, or downright terrified, be able to tap into that inner cheerleader who says, "I've got my own back, even if it feels like no one else does"?

TAKING OWNERSHIP OF YOUR WORDS

"Speaking your truth" sounds wonderful, doesn't it? But it doesn't always lead to nods of agreement. There's no guarantee of a positive response. Sometimes, even when you lay it all out, the response isn't what you hoped for. And this is another thing I want to normalize in this book because it will help you manage your expectations, and hopefully liberate your mind and tongue along the way. The real courage? It's in knowing that your words might stir the pot and choosing to speak anyway. It's about the willingness to face that reality, and voicing what is true—especially when you do so with the guidance of your values and your refined social filter. That is the bravery of speaking out. This is where the concept of ownership mentality becomes another useful tool for you to get acquainted with. It's essentially what we've been unpeeling the layers of in this pillar of Responsibility, but the more specific we can get, the better. Ownership mentality is about taking, well, full *ownership* for your words and their impact, without being overly attached to how they're received.

I like this term because it's an easy one to reach out for when you find yourself placing more focus on what's happening outside of you. It's about understanding that, while you can control your message and its delivery, the response it gets is often beyond your control—which is something I've had to make peace with when it comes to my work, and especially in writing this book. This mindset helps in managing expectations and in freeing your expression from the fear of negative reactions. When you speak with a voice, guided by strong *values* and a nuanced understanding of social dynamics, you embody the essence of *ownership* mentality. You're not just throwing words into the wind; you're carefully crafting and owning your narrative, regardless of the outcome. This approach to communication is what sets apart impactful speakers and leaders, and it's exactly what allows them to create a robust reputation with themselves. In the story of Akeyo, an activist client of mine, that follows, you'll see how this ownership mentality plays out in an undoubtedly challenging scenario.

A few years ago, Akeyo was invited to be a keynote speaker at a high-profile seminar in San Francisco. This extraordinary Kenyan woman has been an on-the-ground advocate against domestic violence and female genital mutilation for over thirty years. She excitedly prepared a talk that was challenging, provocative, and, in my opinion, much needed; something she had done hundreds of times. As she geared up to deliver it, she decided to spotlight the urgent need for diverse voices and open dialogue in her field. One of her strongly held positions was that domestic violence and other forms of sex-based violence weren't just "women's issues." Men are integral, both as allies and as people who face such violence themselves. She felt that sidelining them from these discussions, a trend seen among some Western activists, could slow down the movement's progress. As someone who deeply valued inclusivity, she couldn't see the sense in excluding men from the conversation, no matter how uncomfortable it might be. Akeyo warned of the dangers of muffling voices that offer different perspectives. But what would later cause a stir was her comment about the need to understand the harsh realities of sex-based violence in places outside the Western world. She pointed out that in many non-Western cultures, the difference between gender and sex is crucial, and that conflating these concepts could inadvertently cause more harm. Her take on this sensitive and complicated issue of gender identity led to some people accusing her of being transphobic. This perspective, one that didn't fit neatly into what was deemed the "right" way to think, ignited a firestorm.

On the day of the seminar, Akeyo stood before the audience, took a deep breath, and delivered her talk with all the passion and conviction she could muster. A well-practiced and credible speaker, she was no stranger to delivering thought-provoking speeches to large and focused audiences all over the world. As she delved into her points, she noticed some unrest in the crowd, whispers, and uncomfortable shuffling. She remained focused, finished her speech, and walked off the stage to polite applause. But something didn't feel quite right…

Later that day, she logged on to her social media accounts and was met with a flood of negative comments and messages. She was being called out for promoting "hateful ideas" and for being a "transphobe"; some went as far as accusing her of being an "apologist for abusers" due to her statements on including men in necessary dialogue. She faced severe harassment and criticism from those who interpreted her views as undermining the transgender community and women's issues. There were countless angry messages, with many sharing parts of her speech out of context, twisting her words and misrepresenting her.

Soon after, the seminar organizers sent her an email. They apologized for any upset caused, but distanced themselves from Akeyo's opinions. Her call for open discussion had been misinterpreted as harmful and out of line. What she had intended as a passionate plea for intellectual diversity and open dialogue when it came to sex-based violence had been perceived as a threat, something offensive and unacceptable.

However, the kicker was that most of the loudest critics hadn't even listened to her entire speech or understood that Akeyo had been working closely with the LGBTQ community, including transgender individuals, in Kenya for decades. These communities shared similar concerns to the ones she raised. Assumptions were made without considering her extensive background and experience in these sensitive areas.

Akeyo felt alone, misunderstood, and exiled from the field she had dedicated her life to. Naturally, she felt scared and upset for a short, but intense, time. But she also saw a chance to face it head-on and create an opportunity—an opportunity for dialogue, understanding, and evolution. She found out about me and asked for my help to address the criticism. She returned to her platforms and publicly explained her views, making it clear she wasn't apologizing (more on this shortly), but was open to discussing it further.

Gradually, opinions started shifting. Even if some didn't agree with her, they valued her openness to talk, listen, and understand. She had deep, impactful discussions. Some realized they had been quick to judge and admired her bravery in tackling a touchy subject.

I share this story with you because it's a master class in carving out an unbreakable self-reputation. It's about standing tall in a chorus of doubt and staring misunderstandings square in the face. Sound like a challenge? That's because it is! Remember the insights from the chapters in Part 1: Awareness? We naturally yearn to fit in and, when our views aren't popular, it's tempting to pull the plug on ourselves. When our stance goes against the grain, the easiest path is to second-guess ourselves. I want you to make a declaration that you will not be doing that anymore. It's why drilling down into your core values and holding your ground with conviction is nonnegotiable. And it's not just about the face you present to the world. It's about how you talk to yourself in the mirror, be it your actual mirror or the mirror in your mind.

If you continue to echo what's popular, how will we ever hear your fresh, transformative ideas? If you always choose the safe, easy route, you lose the brilliant colors and sounds of diverse thoughts— including your own. Your discussions become plain and predictable.

When you speak with a voice guided by strong *values* and a nuanced understanding of social dynamics, you embody the essence of *ownership* mentality.

Akeyo learned this the hard way. She realized that voicing unpopular opinions can be risky. Your words can be taken out of context, and facing a crowd of critics can be daunting. But this experience made her value open conversations *even more*. It taught her about the beauty of listening and learning, even from those who don't see eye to eye with you. Most of all, it reminded her that staying silent, simply out of fear, means missing out on chances to evolve, learn, and truly connect with others.

Right on the heels of Akeyo's story, which is a prime example of building a resilient self-reputation and practicing ownership mentality, let's dive into an exercise that will help you do just that. It's time to tackle your own self-reputation head-on. Let's make sure that it's built on a foundation of your true beliefs and values, not just the opinions and expectations of others. This exercise is about reinforcing your inner strength and understanding how to balance external feedback with your internal compass. Ready to challenge yourself and sharpen your self-awareness? Let's get into it.

REPUTATION REINFORCEMENT

External Versus Internal Pressures
- Write down the groups or environments that have a big impact on how you see yourself (like social media, your friends, or work). How do these external voices shape the way you think about who you are?
- Now, write down your own beliefs and the thoughts that come from within you. How do these influence your self-view?

Feedback Processing
- Think of a time when someone criticized you or didn't agree with you. How did it make you react internally? Did it change the way you view yourself or your beliefs?

- On the flip side, remember a moment of praise or affirmation. Did it align with how you see yourself? How did it influence your self-reputation?

Navigating the Maze of Public Perception (a Visualization)

This visualization is hands down one of the most powerful tools I use with clients because it helps you step away from the conscious mind and creatively engage with the idea of overcoming societal judgments.

- **Visualize a Maze:** Imagine yourself at the entrance of a complex maze representing society's judgments and opinions. You are about to enter.

- **Place Personal Symbols:** As you walk through the maze, visualize placing symbols representing your core values, personal beliefs, and strengths. These could be anything from a shield (for resilience), an anchor (for stability), or a compass (for guidance).

- **Identify Challenges and Supports:** Along the maze, visualize drawing obstacles (for example, a wall of thorns for criticism or a mirage for misleading praise) and support elements (like a guiding light for mentorship or a bridge for understanding).

- **Emerge Transformed:** With a pen and paper, sketch yourself coming out of the maze, stronger and more empowered.

- **Reflect on Your Experience:** Consider the challenges you encountered and the tools and support that helped you through. How has navigating this maze changed your perception of handling societal pressures? Does the exit version of you feel more equipped to maintain a true self-reputation amid external influences?

Actionable Commitments

Developing Honest Expression:
- Practice daily reflection, where you spend 10–15 minutes writing down your true thoughts and feelings about a current event or personal experience. This helps in understanding and articulating your genuine perspectives.
- Choose one topic each week that you feel strongly about and plan to share your views on it in a group setting, whether it's a family dinner, a meeting with friends, or a discussion forum online. Prepare key points in advance to help articulate your stance clearly.

Reducing Influence from Outside Noise:
- Schedule regular "unplugged" periods. Start with an hour a day free from digital devices and social media to disconnect from the bombardment of external opinions and focus on your own thoughts.
- Commit to a weekly "mindfulness" activity—like a meditation session, a quiet walk in nature, or yoga—to center yourself and cultivate inner peace. This can rapidly decrease the impact of external feedback.

Detaching from Outside Judgments:
- Arrange a monthly "reality-check" meeting with a close friend or family member where you can discuss and evaluate the opinions and judgments you've encountered recently. I do this with my dear friend Roxanne. Use this as a brave space to express doubts and seek honest feedback.
- Start a personal journal to track instances where you feel swayed by external judgments. Reflect on these moments and write down how you could respond differently in the future, aligning more closely with your true self.

DO NOT BE BULLIED INTO APOLOGIZING

In this vital section of the book, we delve into the nuanced topic I teased earlier: apologies. This exploration is crucial for everyone. Why? Because understanding *when* and *how* to apologize and, most importantly, *why* you are apologizing is integral to building a strong sense of self. This awareness is deeply connected to the principles of responsibility and self-reputation.

The line between genuine self-reflection and coerced conformity has become blurred in the age of instant reactions and digital judgments. How you handle the pressure to apologize, especially when it feels forced upon you, can significantly impact how you perceive yourself and how others perceive you. This isn't just an issue for celebrities or public figures; it's relevant to anyone who engages with others, be it on social media or in face-to-face interactions.

We all know that a misplaced comment or an unconventional view can unleash a flood of backlash, which often leads many people to reactively apologize—not out of sincerity, but to calm the angry mob. There is a serious danger here to our ability to speak to each other. What I'll first make clear is that I'm all for sincere apologies. They play a big role in how we communicate and resolve problems. They're like bridges that help us fix things when relationships go a bit sideways. They let us say, "I messed up." A genuine apology can be powerful. I never want to take a binary "either–or" approach when it comes to this—or any of the work we are doing together. Apologizing, in the true spirit of The Third Perspective, is not about conforming to outside pressures or placating the masses. It's about taking responsibility for your actions when they genuinely conflict with your values or harm others. It's an acknowledgment of your humanity and fallibility, and a commitment to personal growth and empathy. But if someone pushes you into saying sorry, especially if you're just scared, that apology loses its real meaning. An apology loses its potency when it is bullied out of someone.

Now, there are times when we should think twice before saying sorry. Don't just say it to calm a crowd, especially if deep down you feel you haven't done anything wrong. This doesn't mean being stubborn or thinking you're always right. Your resistance should not be born out of ego, self-righteousness, or the unwillingness to be corrected. It's about looking inside yourself, being honest, and understanding where you're coming from.

Imagine you shared an opinion that's close to your heart—a perspective shaped by your experiences, beliefs, and values. Maybe it's different from what a lot of people think and doesn't neatly align with the approved narrative. Perhaps something comes to mind as you read these words. Some people get upset and want an apology. In fact, they don't just want it, they are demanding it. If you genuinely feel your words weren't harmful, you might decide not to apologize just because some people disagree. Having different opinions is part of what makes our communities diverse and vibrant. But remember, standing by your words isn't about ignoring others—it's about respecting different ideas.

It's essential to double-check your reasons for not apologizing. Ask yourself if you're just being stubborn or if there's something more. Dive deep and challenge your own thinking. Listen to what others are saying and try to see things from their viewpoint. One thing to keep in mind is "intellectual humility"—understanding that you don't know everything and can learn from others. It's about being sure of your beliefs while staying open to the idea that you might not have all the answers. Keeping this balance helps you avoid getting too stuck in your ways or letting your ego take over.

If you're always saying sorry when you don't need to, it will chip away at your sense of self. This is a point I always emphasize when talking to my clients and audiences. And it's one I will highlight with you. Unnecessary apologies *take* more than they *give*.

Understanding when
and how to apologize
and, most importantly,
why you are apologizing
is integral to building a
strong sense of self.

It's time now for some introspection. These next statements are designed to help you think through how you express yourself, deal with disagreements, and figure out when saying sorry is the right move. They're a chance for you to really think about how you react and what choices you make when your views bump up against someone else's.

TEN REFLECTION STATEMENTS: APOLOGIES AND YOU

1. "I've apologized for an opinion because I wanted to avoid an argument, even though I still believed in it."
2. "I've felt the urge to say sorry just because my view was different from the popular stance."
3. "I've expressed regret for sharing a personal experience that others didn't relate to."
4. "I've been made to feel that I should apologize for my background or the way I see the world."
5. "I've questioned if I should apologize for a deeply held belief that didn't align with the majority."
6. "I've found myself rehearsing apologies in my head before even speaking out on a topic."
7. "I've caught myself saying 'I'm sorry' for asking questions or seeking clarity on a matter."
8. "I've felt pressure to retract or apologize for a statement that I knew was factually correct."
9. "I've considered issuing a public apology online due to the weight of collective disagreement, even if I wasn't convinced I was wrong."
10. "I've felt that my personal values and worldview are consistently on 'trial,' making me contemplate whether I should apologize for them."

AFTER REFLECTING ON THESE STATEMENTS:

- **Spot the Patterns:** Think about when and why you've felt nudged to say sorry. Did certain situations or places make you feel this way more often? Knowing these patterns helps you prepare for them.
- **Draw Your Boundaries:** Remember those times when you felt pushed to apologize? Think about how you can stand your ground next time. Maybe it's about spending less time in certain online spaces, or maybe it's about telling friends, "I respect your view, but I see things differently."
- **Take Action:** Choose one or two steps you can take to stay true to yourself. Maybe it's finding a group that shares your views or deciding to take a break when online debates get too heated.
- **Gain Perspective:** Share your thoughts with a close friend or mentor, if you feel comfortable doing so. Their input can offer fresh insights and ways to stay genuine in your expressions.

With these steps, you'll not just think about your feelings but also find ways to stay grounded in your integrity, even when the pressure's on.

In a world where people quickly jump to conclusions, sometimes the bravest thing you can do is stand by what you believe, learn from discussions, and always be open to growing and adjusting your viewpoints. And don't forget to be compassionate with yourself, too. Sometimes, we're our biggest critics. (By sometimes, I mean most of the time.) The pressure you put on yourself, worrying about how others view you, can be even more intense than the feedback from others. This inner pressure—the "inner mob" we met in Chapter 2—can push you to hide in sneaky ways.

This inner tug-of-war is influenced by all the expectations and rules you've grown up with and internalized—your personal list of "dos" and "don'ts" from society, fears of being judged, and the chase for social acceptance. When you hide your real thoughts or don't share your changing views, it's like you're apologizing to this inner voice. To bridge the gap between what you feel inside and how you act outside, you need to push yourself. This means thinking about all those internal rules you've set for yourself and seeing whether they still make sense today. It's about accepting that your beliefs can have different layers, and understanding that growing sometimes means changing. You need to have the guts to show your *true* self, even if you're scared of how others—or even you yourself—might react.

PREEMPTIVE APOLOGIES

You're in a meeting, and you have a solution to a big problem that's been troubling your team. But instead of stating it assertively, you begin with, "I might be wrong here, but…" It's not only about the words you're saying, but you also avoid eye contact and fold your body into itself as you speak quietly. (Remember what we said about the importance of body language in Chapter 7?) The result? Your idea doesn't have the impact it could have. Because you hesitated, your team might not even give it a second thought. Instead of standing out, you've unintentionally made your own idea seem less valid.

We all understand the sting of missed opportunities, like that job you didn't go for or that conversation you avoided. I sure do. But have you ever thought about the price of constantly saying "sorry" (even with your demeanor) when you don't need to, or communicating passively? We dived into your communication style in Chapter 7, and I want to tap back into it here. It's crucial, as it shapes how you see yourself. It has everything to do with your self-reputation.

Think about everyday life. Because we worry about offending others, we often end up walking on eggshells. By always trying to be

You need to have the guts
to show your *true* self,
even if you're scared of
how others—or even you
yourself—might react.

cautious, we end up weakening our words. All those extra disclaimers, qualifiers, and "sorrys" might seem like we're just trying to be polite, but, in reality, we're watering down our own message and showing that we doubt ourselves. We're stripping our words of their power. This isn't just about work or casual conversations. In close relationships, if you're always holding back or being overly careful, it might seem like everything's okay on the surface. But underneath, there could be misunderstandings or unspoken feelings brewing. Instead of truly connecting and sorting things out in times of conflict, we may just be glossing over issues.

Now, when you take this to the digital realm, the stakes get even higher. Social media lets everyone voice their thoughts. But out of fear of being dogpiled in the comments, you might sugarcoat your real opinions, making them lose their genuine feel. I see this happen time and time again. Ever hesitated before posting something online? Wanted to share a thought, a story, or an experience, but added so many conditions to it that the real essence got lost? Or maybe decided not to post at all?

The outcome of this is that your online presence doesn't truly reflect your genuine thoughts. It lacks that distinct touch, which could lead to deeper connections or start insightful discussions. Constantly toning down your words and using "preemptive apologies" can slowly eat away at your self-belief. When the language you use keeps *implying* that your views might not be that important or worthy, you start believing it! This can cause you to hold back even when it's crucial to speak out.

So, what's the solution?

Realizing the weight of this is the first big step. It's not about going to the other extreme and being confrontational, it's about striking a balance. It's about sharing your thoughts honestly and assertively, without always cushioning them with disclaimers. Your voice is important, and it's high time you recognized its true value.

When the language you
use keeps *implying* that
your views might not be
that important or worthy,
you start believing it!

The repeatedly added "I'm sorry, but…" or "Just thinking out loud here, but…" might appear as mere politeness or caution. But in reality, they sow seeds of doubt within you. These unneeded apologies can feel like shackles, making you question your very own beliefs and thoughts. And each "This might not be right, but…" or "Hope this doesn't upset anyone, but…" erodes your confidence—slowly but surely. It's essential to recognize this pattern, so you don't get trapped in a loop of constant self-doubt.

The following exercise will support you in rethinking your apology habits, both offline and online.

BREAKING FREE FROM PASSIVE COMMUNICATION OFFLINE

Step 1: Track Your Apologies
- **Task:** For a single day, make a note every time you use preemptive apologies or disclaimers in your conversations—this will be your apology log.
- **Why It Helps:** This will help you realize just how much you use "softening" phrases in your communication. We tend to be unaware of how often we subconsciously water down and undermine our statements. No more!

Step 2: Practice Assertive Restatement
- **Task:** Revisit your apology log and choose a few typical statements. Reformulate them to remove the apologies so that your core message remains.
- **Examples:**
  o **Before:** "I might be wrong, but I think we should reconsider our marketing strategy."
  o **After:** "I believe we should reconsider our marketing strategy."

Step 3: Question Your Fear

- **Task:** Every time you're about to use an unnecessary apology, pause. Reflect on the underlying emotion.
- **Reflective Questions:**
  o What's triggering this apology?
  o Am I genuinely remorseful, or am I trying to avoid potential disagreement or judgment?

Step 4: Role-Play for Practice

- **Task:** Team up with a trusted friend or family member. Let them set up various situations where you typically use passive communication. Engage in these scenarios and aim to respond without your usual disclaimers or apologies. Relax into it and engage fully.
- **Why It Helps:** Practicing in a safe, nonjudgmental environment can build your confidence and make you more aware of your default communication patterns.

Remember: Change doesn't happen overnight. By committing to this deep reflection, and following through with action, you're learning to speak your truth with real conviction—rather than just saying sorry to keep everyone happy. This way of thinking, central to The Third Perspective, is all about striking the right balance—it's standing strong in what you believe while *staying open* to new ideas and understanding. As you get better at speaking up without always leaning on apologies you don't really mean, your conversations will start to change. YOU will start to change. Your interactions will become more honest, more meaningful, and more positive and worthwhile for everyone involved.

COMBATING APOLOGETIC MESSAGING ON SOCIAL MEDIA

Step 1: Social Media Audit

- **Action:** Take a look at your past social media posts or comments.
- **Goal:** Do a thorough review and spot instances of passive language or unnecessary disclaimers.
- **Reflection:** Understand why you felt the need to add these and consider how they might've changed the message's overall impact.

Step 2: Clear and Concise

- **Action:** Practice formulating your ideas in a clear and to-the-point manner.
- **Tip:** Skip qualifiers or disclaimers that weaken your message. Your opinions are valid; own them.

Step 3: Mindful Posting

- **Action:** Before hitting "post," evaluate your word choice.
- **Question:** Are any added disclaimers or apologies truly needed? Or is there something you're afraid of?

Step 4: Engage Constructively

- **Action:** When confronted with opposing views, opt for a constructive dialogue.
- **Tip:** Understand the other's viewpoint, but articulate your perspective with confidence. No need for apologies.

Step 5: Don't Fear Mistakes

- **Action:** Accept that you won't always get it right.
- **Insight:** If a post is found to be off-mark or insensitive, recognize the oversight, learn, and move forward. Every opinion or mistake is part of the learning process.

When you challenge passive messaging on all your platforms, it allows you to fully embrace the potential of social media. You can make room for better connections, an environment where sharing ideas can be exciting and expansive, and you create a space for exchanges that inspire and expand you.

Before we wrap up this chapter, I want to take a moment to acknowledge your journey so far. You've walked through the complexities of self-awareness and responsibility, and, now, you stand on the threshold of the final pillar: Expression. This is where you lay it all out on the table, getting crystal clear about what you're willing to risk for the sake of aligning more closely with the person you are becoming.

As you step into this next phase, remember: your voice, your story, your truth—they're yours to articulate. The Expression pillar is not just about speaking up; it's about owning your narrative with conviction and clarity. It's where you define your terms, set your boundaries, and declare your stance with unapologetic authenticity. This is your chance to really shine, to show the world the depths and nuances of who you are.

You've come a long way, and now it's time to harness all that you've learned, to embolden your voice and make it heard. Imagine the possibilities when you fully embrace your unique perspective and share it openly. Think about the connections you'll forge, the dialogues you'll spark, and the impact you can make.

So as you prepare to dive into the world of Expression, do so with a heart full of courage and a mind open to endless possibilities. This is your moment to redefine the narrative, to step into your power, and to TELL PEOPLE WHO YOU ARE. Let your voice ring out, clear and true, in this vibrant, ever-evolving world. The stage is yours—speak your truth and watch as the world listens.

PART 3

Expression:

WHAT ARE YOU WILLING TO RISK?

You are now in the liberating realm of saying what you really feel, even when it's not the popular opinion. In this part of your journey through *The Third Perspective*, you're shaking off the worry about what others think and reactivating the courage to stand tall in your own views. You'll start by awakening the maverick within you—that bold, fearless side of you that's been waiting for its moment. Imagine not stumbling over your words in a challenging conversation, but speaking clearly and confidently, because you know exactly where you stand. This is the place where you'll learn to have those honest exchanges, even if your voice shakes a little at first.

But all these lessons need a testing ground. You'll be urged to "enter the arena" of real-world interactions, far removed from the distant corridors of social media. You'll be guided to cultivate a realistic and sustainable path to integrate all that you have learned into your daily life, stretching beyond your comfort zones but within the bounds of your well-being. It's all about building a solid ground for yourself, one step at a time, where being you isn't just okay, it's celebrated.

As you come to the end of this book, picture reintroducing yourself to the world, but this time, without holding anything back. Feel the exhilaration of being completely you, without the filters and without the fear. You're about to open a door to a life that's a whole lot richer, braver, and, best of all, exciting.

Chapter 10

Unleash Your Inner Maverick

Courage. It's a word that might conjure up images of super-heroes, a firefighter rushing into a burning building, a leader standing up to make a speech that could change the course of history, an epic battle. But let's bring it back down to earth. It's also in the small, everyday choices that push you out of your comfort zone. It's about speaking up in a meeting when it's easier to stay quiet or admitting you were wrong when you could've just walked away. Courage isn't about being fearless or having some kind of superpower. It's about feeling the fear and deciding something else is more important. It's the choice to move forward, even when every part of you is saying it's easier to stand still.

And here's a crucial insight: courage isn't something you inherit, etched into your DNA—it's not set in stone. Think of it more like a skill you can develop, something that grows with each step you take. It's something everyone has, but you've got to use it to make it strong. It's about cultivating that inner strength that lets you persevere (that's grit), building the mental and emotional toughness to face life's hard-ships (we call that fortitude), and learning to recover quickly from difficulties (that's resilience). It's a practice—just like learning to play an instrument or training for a marathon. And every time you choose to face a challenge instead of avoiding it, you're giving that courage muscle a workout.

Now, let's talk about the maverick mindset. Mavericks are the trailblazers, the ones who color outside the lines and march to the beat of their own drum. They don't wait for someone else to give them permission to act. The maverick mindset is about embracing that same spirit within yourself. This is where you recognize that you have the power to make choices that align with your values, even if those choices go against the grain.

The maverick mindset is fueled by a quality of courage that's conscious and deliberate. It's the kind that says, "I see the risk, I feel the fear, and yet, I choose to move forward because my beliefs, my voice, and my actions matter." This mindset doesn't rely on bravado or recklessness; it's rooted in a clear sense of purpose and a commitment to authenticity.

To fire up the bravery that's already in you, you've got to grow a maverick mindset. Imagine mixing up a bit of do-it-your-own-way attitude, some out-of-the-box thinking, a dash of daring, and a good chunk of bounce-back toughness. That's the maverick mindset. It's for those who aren't scared to question how things are usually done, who like to think differently, and who can stand their ground, even if it means standing by themselves.

KEY ASPECTS OF A MAVERICK MINDSET

- **Independent Thinking:** You think for yourself and are not easily swayed by public opinion. You value your autonomy in thought and are often skeptical of conventional wisdom if it doesn't hold up to scrutiny.
- **Innovative and Creative:** You see opportunities where others see obstacles and are not afraid to try new approaches or ideas. Mavericks are often associated with innovation because they approach problems and solutions differently from the majority.

- **Risk-Taking:** Mavericks are willing to take calculated risks. You understand that to achieve something great, you must step out of your comfort zone and embrace the possibility of failure.
- **Resilience and Perseverance:** When faced with setbacks, mavericks are resilient. You bounce back from failures and view them as learning experiences rather than insurmountable defeats.
- **Authenticity:** You are true to yourself and your values. Mavericks are not interested in pretending to be something they're not, even if authenticity comes at the cost of popularity.
- **Non-Conformity:** This is a big one! You do not conform for the sake of conformity. You have the courage to challenge norms and traditions that you believe are outdated or wrong.
- **Passionate Conviction:** Mavericks are often deeply passionate about their pursuits. Your conviction drives you to persist where others might give up.
- **Visionary Outlook:** You can often see the bigger picture and have a clear vision of what you want to achieve. Mavericks are driven by a sense of purpose that guides their actions.
- **Charismatic Leadership:** Many mavericks are charismatic leaders, inspiring others with their conviction and steadfastness. You lead by example and often rally others to your cause.
- **Strategic and Calculated:** While you may seem to act against the grain, your actions are often well thought out and strategic. You think several steps ahead and are tactical in your approach to challenges.
- **Adaptability:** Mavericks are adaptable and thrive in changing environments. You are quick to adjust your strategies to meet new circumstances.

If these aspects of the maverick feel worlds away from who you are right now, take heart. That's exactly why you're here. You're on the cusp of waking up that courage inside you, that muscle we've been talking about, ready to flex and grow. It's about stepping out of the usual routine and daring to do things a little—or a lot—differently.

You might be thinking, "That's not me. I can't just change who I am." But the truth is, you're not changing who you are; you're *becoming* more of who you're meant to be. You're not *transforming* into someone else; you're letting the real you take center stage—the *you* that's been waiting for permission to speak up, to act, to live boldly. This is your green light.

SETTING THE EMOTIONAL STAGE FOR YOUR INNER MAVERICK

Ever witnessed someone fearlessly speaking their mind, voicing their beliefs, and radiating confidence while they're at it? While watching them, did you feel a mix of awe, envy, and perhaps a tinge of annoyance, without even knowing why? If this resonates with you, know you're in good company. Activating your maverick mindset starts with examining why these feelings tend to come to the surface. In my experience this happens when we stifle our inner maverick—the raw, unfiltered version of ourselves that is crying out for expression. It's the free spirit inside all of us that's sick and tired of being left out. When you silence it, it's as though you're living two lives. There's the facade you present to society, and then there's your hidden true essence. And the longer you hide, the more out of touch and fraudulent you feel.

Seeing people who fully embrace their maverick side highlights this gap. They're not just role models; they're like mirrors showing you the authenticity and values you've pushed aside. And if you and I are going to really talk about Expression, this is something we can't ignore. It's not their boldness that unsettles you; it's the freedom they display—a freedom you've kept locked up inside. Feeling this way isn't just about not liking them; it's about missing the brave, audacious part of yourself. When you don't take this as a sign to lean into

You're not changing who you are; you're *becoming* more of who you're meant to be. You're not *transforming* into someone else; you're letting the real you take center stage.

your own courage, this can lead you to become more judgmental, skeptical, and withdrawn, which in turn cuts you off from making real connections and strengthening your confidence muscle. You might notice it in everyday situations, like when a colleague confidently pitches a new idea at work while you hold back your own, or when a friend in a social gathering shares a controversial opinion with ease, and you choose silence to avoid any disagreement. It's apparent in the way some people present their unfiltered selves on social media, making you second-guess your hesitation to post anything too personal or controversial. Or in family settings, when a relative always speaks their mind on sensitive issues, while you prefer to keep your true opinions under wraps to keep the peace. Even witnessing artists or writers who fearlessly explore bold themes can highlight your own hesitance in expressing unconventional ideas. Each of these instances shows the conflict between the boldness you see in others and the restraint you've imposed on yourself.

Throughout the years, I've had many people confess that their initial encounter with my work brought about strong feelings of resistance, even feeling "triggered." Some unfollowed me, others muted my posts, or they simply felt an unsettling disconnect and were quick to decide that my message wasn't for them. But then, they kept coming back, almost like they couldn't help it, sneaking peeks to see what I was saying next. There was something in the way I presented my ideas—perhaps it was my spirited energy, my steadfast belief in my message, the way I'd openly share, or my knack for mixing in a bit of humor—that captured their interest like a part of themselves they had yet to recognize. I get where they're coming from because I've been there too.

When you quiet that inner trailblazer, that gutsy part of you, it's like you're saying you don't believe in your own intuition. You start putting more weight on what others think than on what you know deep down. If you keep it up, that inner voice gets harder to hear, and you start losing touch with the real you. Looking back at the days leading up to me publishing my open letter, I can tell you that even though I was nervous and had more than a few doubts, something inside me kept pushing me to go through with it. Now I can see it was instrumental in pushing me toward a major turning point. My need to let the truth roll off my tongue grew stronger than the worries that used to hold me down by my shoulders.

On my own path, I've come across people who were out there, loud and proud about what they believed in. A lot of the time, they were saying things that hit home for me, too. But, if I'm being honest, there were moments when I'd pick apart the tiniest things they said or did. Looking back, I can see that this nitpicking came from a place of envy and insecurity. These people were out there, not just talking the talk, but walking the walk with their beliefs. And after a while, I got it—their boldness wasn't something to get defensive about or feel threatened by; it was a gift! They were showing me the ropes of possibility. Instead of sticking with my knee-jerk reactions, I began to see their example as a kick in the pants to up my own game—to turn all that envy into drive and fire.

The people I looked up to, the ones whose traits I admired, weren't as far off from me as I'd thought. All those awkward, messy feelings made me believe that I couldn't be like them, and luckily I got to discover that they were wrong. If you've ever felt like you're miles away from having the characteristics that the courageous embody, here's something to remember: All those tough emotions you're wrestling with? They're not your enemies. They're pretty useful. Like the mob in your mind, they can be your allies. If you face up to those "wrong thoughts" head-on, you can get in touch with your own inner maverick. That part of you that thinks for itself, that's not afraid to speak up and stand strong. Let the following exercise help you to spot those times when someone's bravery stirred strong feelings in you.

UNCOVERING HIDDEN DESIRES

You may occasionally come across people who bravely voice their truths, and are willing to go against the grain. Their audacity can bring up a host of emotions within you, from admiration to irritation and, sometimes, even resentment. Why? Perhaps because they mirror the very qualities you yearn to exhibit. By diving into these emotions, you can find out more about the qualities you secretly wish to have.

Step 1: Recall and Reflect
• Think back to recent interactions, be it in personal conversations, online discussions, or public forums. Identify a moment when someone voiced an opinion or took an action that left a strong impression on you.
• **Describe That Incident Briefly:** Who was it? What did they say or do? How did it deviate from the "accepted" narrative?

Step 2: Analyze Your Reaction
• Detail your immediate emotional response. Did you feel annoyed, defensive, or perhaps even envious? Were you inspired or did you feel an urge to counter their viewpoint?
• **Ask Yourself:** Why did I feel this way? Was it truly about the content of their message, or was it more about the courage they displayed?

Step 3: Identify the Mirror
• Reflect deeply on the characteristic or trait that individual exhibited. Was it their boldness, authenticity, resilience, or maybe their vulnerability?
• **Ask yourself:** Do I wish I could embody that trait more in my life?

198

Step 4: Visualize Embracing the Trait

- Imagine a scenario where you could demonstrate that same trait. What would you say or do? How would it make you feel? Write down steps you can take to nurture and exhibit this characteristic in your life. For instance, if you're struck by someone's fearless approach to challenging popular opinions and you pictured yourself in a group discussion, boldly presenting a viewpoint that goes against the mainstream but reflects your true thoughts, one of the steps you could take could be starting small and sharing your opinions in less formal, more intimate settings. This will help build your confidence in expressing your viewpoints without pressure. It can also make you feel secure and self-assured, which eases your anxiety and nervousness, leading to a more natural expression of your thoughts.

Step 5: Confront and Challenge

- Reflect on societal norms that might discourage you from embracing this trait. Are there unspoken rules or fears holding you back?
- **Challenge Yourself:** Set a small goal to act on this trait in the coming week. It could be sharing an unpopular opinion, standing up for someone/something, or just being open about your feelings.

Every time you encounter people who stir strong emotions within you, check in with yourself and see if it's because they present a mirror to your deepest desires and insecurities. Instead of shying away from these feelings, embrace them. Use them as stepping stones to understand yourself better and to grow into the person you wish to be. After all, every courageous person you meet is an invitation to *awaken* the bravery within you.

Think of that pull, that curiosity, as the maverick spirit being ignited within you. It's that little nudge inside that knows where you're meant to be, even when you feel all tangled up in your own worries.

Releasing your inner maverick means making a commitment to face the things that scare you. It's being truthful and standing up for what's right, even if you stand alone. It's about making the choice, again and again, to step into the arena of your life, back straightened, ready to fully engage.

This is where I tell you that it's okay to start small. I'm reminded of one of my favorite quotes by Mary Anne Radmacher from *Courage Doesn't Always Roar*: "Sometimes courage is the quiet voice at the end of the day saying, 'I will try again tomorrow.'" But you will not use this as an excuse to stay stagnant. Those small decisions build up like layers, forming the strong foundation of a maverick mindset. Each choice to be brave, each moment you step out of the shadows, you're lighting a spark that can turn into a wildfire of change.

Now, let me show you what creating the brave environments you crave looks like in action. Here you commit to making a space where you can be the truest version of yourself while inspiring others to do the same. And there's no better example of this than the story of Malala Yousafzai...

CREATE THE BRAVE ENVIRONMENTS YOU CRAVE

In a small corner of Pakistan, there was a girl named Malala Yousafzai who stood up for something you and I might not think twice about: going to school. Where she lived, girls were often kept out of class-rooms, but Malala loved to learn and wouldn't take "no" for an answer. She started writing a blog without using her real name, talking about her dreams of education and how tough life was under the strict rules of the Taliban. People all over the world started to follow her stories, opening their eyes to what was going on. But this also put her in *great* danger.

Every courageous person you meet is an invitation to *awaken* the bravery within you.

One day, when Malala was on her way back from school, a gunman from the Taliban shot her in the head, with the goal being silencing her once and for all. But Malala didn't let that stop her. She fought through and, with a courage that amazed everyone, she survived and kept fighting—not just for herself, but for girls everywhere to get the education they deserve. She became the youngest Nobel Peace Prize laureate, showing us all what it means to believe in something so much that you're willing to fight for it, no matter what. Malala taught us that, sometimes, one person standing up for what's right can start a wave of change. She wanted a world where every kid could go to school, and she made that fight her own. I'm not sharing Malala's story simply to inspire you—it's a reminder of how brave and creative the human spirit can be when it's fighting for what's right.

Malala's bravery reminds me of another story, one that hits closer to home.

Meet my friend Miles. He's an up-and-coming writer who never shies away from shaking things up with his prose. Miles doesn't play it safe; he's the guy who'll call it like he sees it, especially in his writing. Calling it how he sees it is exactly what he did when he decided to take a hard look at a super-popular book series. He pointed out how it didn't do a great job with women's roles and wasn't too hot on diversity either.

Even though Miles was extremely thoughtful and balanced in his critique, his words stirred up a hornet's nest. The fans of the book series weren't happy. Instead of engaging with the content of what he was saying, they launched a social media campaign against him. Like Akeyo's story in Chapter 9, they twisted his words, attacking his character and painting him as "an enemy of art." He was accused of "going woke." A little dramatic if you ask me. Miles tried to get a real conversation going, but all he got back was a wall of noise and anger. It hit him hard. He started to play it safe with his writing, sticking to topics that wouldn't get people riled up again.

But just when it looked like Miles had lost his creative edge and might never take another risk with his words, something amazing happened. Out of the blue, he got an email from this famous writer he's always looked up to. This writer had read his critique and actually liked it. They started talking and, the next thing you know, Miles was asked to write the introduction for the writer's new book.

That chance encounter with a respected author was just the spark Miles needed. It reminded him that his opinions mattered, even if they went against the grain. Fired up by this, he made a choice: no more letting fear call the shots. He went back to his original no-holds-barred way of writing. Sure, not everyone liked it, but there were plenty of people out there who really got into his fresh takes and the way he made them think. But Miles didn't just stop with getting his own groove back. He saw the bigger picture. He knew there had to be others out there who felt just as boxed in, worried about getting slammed for their ideas. So, he set out to create a space where anyone could say what they wanted to say, a place I'm proud to be part of. It's a community where wild (never extreme), bold thoughts are welcome, and no one has to tone it down for fear of social punishment.

Miles began with just a handful of bold writers he looked up to, the kind who weren't afraid to stir the pot with their words. He reached out, shared his own ups and downs, and invited them to share theirs. One by one, this tribe of daring writers started to grow, turning into a close-knit community that had each other's backs and cheered on every challenge to the usual way of thinking.

Think about Malala, standing strong against incredible odds, and Miles, rebuilding his world after it seemed like everyone was against him. They both tell us something important—that when you've got the courage to stand up for what you believe in, you can change the world around you, whether that's for everyone to see or just in your own circle.

The waves these people make keep spreading, changing stories and lives as they go. The same can happen for you. Every time you put your thoughts out there, you're weaving the kind of conversations and groups you wish to see. You've got the power to shake things up and make room for a myriad of voices and ideas. Your voice counts, no matter how "out there" it might seem. And even the tiniest act of bravery from you could be just the nudge someone else needs to unshackle themselves.

You might be thinking, "Starting a whole community, that's a lot." But here's the thing: change doesn't have to start big. You must move away from the stereotypical image that pops up when you think of "bravery." A lot of the time, it can present itself as the quiet strength of sticking to what you believe in. Just one person's brave step can set off a whole wave of change that touches lives far and wide. And guess what? You're part of this too. It can begin with just you and one other person—a friend, a family member, anyone you trust. Think about the times when a good conversation with someone close to you opened your eyes to something new or gave you the activation you needed. That's the power of one-on-one connections.

Find that person in your life who gets you, who cheers you on when you want to say what's on your mind. Sitting down with them, swapping thoughts and worries, and seeing things from their point of view can lay the foundation for the kind of open space you're looking for. This is something I turn to often.

By talking with this person regularly, you'll not only get a deeper understanding of things, but you'll start feeling more confident about sharing your voice with the world. It's like building your own support system, one conversation at a time.

If your mind starts drifting to "I don't have that person or that kind of place to speak freely," then take this as your cue to start exploring. It requires effort on your part, but it's very possible! Surprisingly, you might encounter like-minded individuals in the most unexpected places—it could be in an online group, a local book club, a class you enroll in, or perhaps someone you connect with at a social event.

The tiniest act of bravery from you could be just the nudge someone else needs to unshackle themselves.

To help guide you in this quest, I'll give you a structured plan to build your community where free and open expression is welcomed and encouraged.

CREATING THE BRAVE COMMUNITY YOU DESIRE

- **Identify Your Passion Areas:**
  - o Pinpoint topics, causes, or hobbies that you're truly passionate about or curious to learn more about (for example, environmental activism, creative writing, tech innovations, mental health awareness, culinary arts, free speech advocacy).
  - o Make a list of these interests, as they are the foundations of the communities where open expression thrives.

- **Seek Out Local Platforms:**
  - o Explore local clubs, groups, or events that resonate with your interests, such as book clubs, hobby classes, or community service initiatives.
  - o Attend events and meetups in your area, checking local community boards or online event platforms for opportunities.

- **Dive into Online Communities:**
  - o Discover forums, social media groups, or websites focused on your areas of interest.
  - o Actively participate in discussions, share your insights, and connect with other members.

- **Spark Conversations:**
  - o Initiate discussions in both digital and physical spaces.
  - o Share your thoughts and be open to diverse viewpoints, which will create an environment where all voices are heard.

- **Engage in Educational Events:**
  - o Join workshops, seminars, or talks that align with your interests. These gatherings are hotspots for meeting people who value open dialogue.
  - o Interact with presenters and fellow attendees, creating connections based on shared learning.

- **Follow Up with New Connections:**
  - o Keep in touch with people you meet, whether through a friendly message, email, or casual meetup invitation.
  - o Suggest ideas for future gatherings or discussions that encourage open expression.

- **Establish Your Own Forum or Platform:**
  - o If you don't find a group that suits your needs, take the initiative to create your own, either online or in your local community. This is exactly what I had to do. You can even use this book to start your own book club!
  - o Promote your group to attract individuals who share your interest in open, honest conversations.

- **Stay Actively Involved:**
  - o Regularly engage in group activities and conversations.
  - o Contribute by sharing resources or offering support, enhancing the community's value.

- **Cultivate an Open Environment:**
  - o Nurture a space where respectful and open discussions are the norm.
  - o Support diverse opinions and ideas, enriching the community experience.

- **Continuously Evaluate and Evolve:**
  - o Regularly reflect on your experiences within these communities.
  - o Be ready to modify your approach or seek out new groups to ensure a dynamic and fulfilling community experience.

By following this plan—which again, requires effort on your part—you'll gradually create and become part of communities that appreciate and celebrate open and honest expression, and they will be aligned with your interests and values.

A community is not just going to magically appear in front of you—you need to put yourself forward for it. Courageously. The key is to remain proactive, open-minded, and committed to nurturing yourself *and* these spaces.

The world's a big place with many different views just waiting to be discovered. All you've got to do is gather up a bit of bravery, a willingness to follow through, and set off on the hunt. The next stage on your path to brave expression involves naming the risks you're willing to take, then you will reveal the rewards. Without risk, there is no expression. Without risk, there is no Third Perspective.

Chapter 11

Brave Expression: A Price Worth Paying

You're standing at the edge of a diving board for the very first time. You can feel your heart thumping as you look down at the water way below. It's scary, it's a risk, that jump into the unknown, and everything inside you is shouting, "Just step back where it's safe!" But then there's this little voice that whispers, "If you don't jump, you'll never feel the rush of the dive and the excitement of making a big splash." This is the moment of decision that stands between where you are and where you could be—stay where you've always been or take that leap and see what happens. If you want to be someone who's not afraid to say what they think, or someone who's effective when they *do* say what they think, you've got to be ready to take the plunge. You have to be willing to do something differently.

Taking risks isn't about being reckless or impulsive. It doesn't mean you're throwing caution to the wind or just blurting out whatever comes to mind. It's not about ignoring the possible fallout. It's more about thoughtful decisions, knowing that everything you say adds to how people see you and feeds into the big conversation we're all having as a society.

Here's the hard truth: if you're not ready to be *misunderstood*, to be seen as controversial, or to stand alone at times, then you're gambling away a lot more. You risk getting comfortable with suppressing your voice. The greatest ideas and movements that shook the world started with someone who dared to face the heat of everyone's opinions and tough it out, all for something bigger and better.

There are those who want all the benefits of being brave—the clout, the props, the kind of reputation that lasts. But they're not up for the tough tasks you have to complete before the benefits can be experienced. Do not let that be your story. Standing up and speaking boldly isn't for those who back down easily. It's for the bold ones, the dreamers, the never-give-uppers who truly think their words can make a difference. Be it out there in the world or in the privacy of their own home, it all counts.

Keep in mind that the extent of what you're willing to risk or share is a deeply personal choice and will vary greatly from person to person. What might seem trivial to one person might be a monumental step for someone else. The leap you choose to take could be one of the following, each significant in its own right:

- **Opening Up About Addiction:** Sharing your journey with addiction, whether that's to substances, behaviors, or patterns that have negatively impacted your life and relationships.
- **Revealing an Abusive Relationship:** Discussing experiences in a relationship that may have appeared perfect on the outside, but was abusive or toxic behind closed doors.
- **Sharing Mental Health Struggles:** Opening up about personal battles with depression, anxiety, or other mental health issues, which often come with a lot of stigma.
- **Admitting to Financial Difficulties:** Discussing financial struggles or failures, especially in cultures that equate financial success with personal worth.

If you're not ready to be *misunderstood*, to be seen as controversial, or to stand alone at times, then you're gambling away a lot more.

- **Revealing a Hidden Aspect of Identity:** This could be coming out about your sexual orientation, gender identity, or even lesser-known aspects like being a survivor of a traumatic event.

- **Challenging Cultural or Familial Norms:** Speaking out against long-held traditions or expectations that don't align with your personal beliefs or values.

- **Confessing Failure or Mistakes:** Admitting to a significant mistake at work or in your personal life, especially when there's pressure to appear competent and successful.

- **Discussing Unpopular Opinions on Social Issues:** Sharing views on political, environmental, or social issues that might be contrary to the prevailing opinion in your social circle.

- **Revealing Creative Projects:** Sharing artistic or creative work that is deeply personal to you and might be subject to criticism or misunderstanding.

- **Discussing a Change in Belief Systems:** Opening up about a shift in religious or spiritual beliefs, especially if it's a departure from your family or community norms.

Of course, this list is not exhaustive, but it highlights some of the areas where making a bold choice to speak up or stand out can be particularly impactful.

Each act of bravery, every risk you embrace, proves you don't just talk about courage—you live it. It's simple to stand in the shadow of giants, watch the "big names" do daring things, and applaud them for it. But actually stepping up and being brave yourself? That's tougher, sure, but it's also way more satisfying.

Think of your life like a book you're writing, especially when it comes to how you talk and share your thoughts. Ask yourself: What am I ready to risk? How am I going to handle it when people don't agree with me? How can I speak my mind in a way that's strong but also careful and kind?

My entire body of work focuses on bridging divides in a polarized climate—I am willing to put forward my concerns about the way we often undermine each other, how our society punishes difference and the heavy price we pay when we mute ourselves. Each time I share my writing, create a podcast episode, say yes to interviews on mainstream platforms, or push back on various narratives encouraging victimhood and disempowerment, I'm well aware that my work might come across people who are ready to misunderstand me. This is something I have had to accept. But there was a time when the stakes felt too high. For years, I had seen people being ripped to shreds online for simply asking a question that was filed in the "wrong think" category. I knew that if I chose to speak what I knew to be true, I might be waving goodbye to part of my audience, some of my clients, potential collaborators, and a slice of my professional reputation. And I would be lying if I said that some of that didn't happen. I did indeed have to bid farewell to some of the people in my audience who no longer felt that I represented them and their views. But I welcomed hundreds of thousands of people who were glad to have come across someone willing to call it how they saw it. I was able to align with clients who didn't require me to shapeshift for their comfort.

I had to quickly come to terms with the fact that my comfort zone had never been as safe as I thought. And I'm telling you, letting go of that comfort is the least we can do—it's the very starting point of our journey toward genuine self-expression. I need you to understand that stepping out of your comfort zone is just the beginning, and it's nonnegotiable. This is excellent news.

Even as I wrote this book, I felt that familiar tug of resistance—my inner mob showed up a few times to warn me against risk. Good

Decide that other people's *perception* of you is something you're willing to detach from.

thing I'm friends with them. There were moments when I felt vulnerable, like I was putting "too much" of myself out there. Sometimes, it felt like I was crossing a line, saying things that maybe I shouldn't. I'm sharing this with you because I want to be completely up-front about how tough it can be to walk through the door of bravery. But just like I've done at many points in my life and career, I embraced the risk. Why? Because the message I have—the opportunity to connect, to share, and perhaps to ignite change—will always outweigh the fear.

WHAT ARE *YOU* WILLING TO RISK?

Now, let's talk about you. Remember the discussion we had in the previous chapter about measured courage? Identifying your own threshold for risk, the specifics of what you're willing to put at stake, is a critical step. You won't be charging ahead without thought—you'll be making an informed choice that reflects your principles and your vision for the impact you want to make.

None of what we're doing here comes without risk, and I stand firm in comfort being the bare minimum you can risk. You don't have to risk everything—but you might decide that other people's *perception* of you is something you're willing to detach from, or perhaps it's letting go of mismatched friendships, or losing clients who don't agree with your political opinions.

Risk is essential if you want to meet your growth edge. Yes, it comes with the chance of loss, but the potential gains are immense: greater self-respect, living in harmony with your values, and the profound satisfaction of authenticity. Taking risks that align with your core values isn't just about surviving; it's about truly living. It involves embracing the uncertainties and discovering strength in moments of vulnerability. Consider this: What are you prepared to risk to remain faithful to yourself?

Let's start by looking at the risks you might face and the rewards that can come when you choose to be true to your own voice. The following list will help you weigh up what you might have to navigate and what you stand to gain. It's useful to understand the balance between what you're putting on the line and the personal victories that could be right around the corner. Picture each risk as a hurdle you can clear and every reward as a milestone you reach. There may be challenges scattered along the path, but there's also the promise of finding something truly valuable.

REWARDS OF BRAVE EXPRESSION

- **Personal Integrity:** Staying true to yourself and your values can help you create a strong sense of personal integrity and authenticity.
- **Leadership and Influence:** Brave communicators often become influential voices because they inspire others with their courage and conviction.
- **Social Change:** Expressing controversial or forward-thinking ideas can be a catalyst for social change and progress.
- **Empowerment:** There's a profound sense of empowerment that comes with overcoming the fear of judgment or backlash.
- **Personal Growth:** Engaging in brave expression can lead to significant personal growth, the kind that enhances your confidence and self-esteem.
- **Creating Dialogue:** Brave expression can initiate important conversations, bringing light to overlooked issues.
- **Community-Building:** By speaking out, you can connect with like-minded people and cultivate a sense of community and support.
- **Educational Impact:** Sharing your knowledge or perspective can educate others and broaden collective understanding.
- **Career Advancement:** In some fields (maybe even yours!), the ability to express ideas boldly and effectively can lead to career advancement.

- **Emotional Release:** There's a cathartic release in expressing your emotions and thoughts openly, which can be mentally and emotionally liberating.

RISKS OF BRAVE EXPRESSION

- **Backlash and Criticism:** Voicing your opinion can lead to public criticism, harassment, or backlash, especially in polarized environments.
- **Relationship Strains:** Personal and professional relationships may be strained or damaged if others disagree with or are hurt by your expressed views.
- **Misinterpretation:** There's always a risk of your words being taken out of context or misunderstood, leading to unintended consequences.
- **Professional Repercussions:** In some industries or roles, expressing certain opinions can lead to job loss, demotion, or other professional setbacks.
- **Social Ostracization:** Being vocal about unpopular or controversial views can sometimes lead to social exclusion or marginalization.
- **Legal Consequences:** In extreme cases, especially in environments with strict laws on speech, brave expression can lead to legal issues.
- **Personal Safety:** Depending on the context and the content of the expression, there can be a risk to your personal safety.
- **Emotional Toll:** The stress of facing opposition and navigating conflict can take an emotional toll on individuals.
- **Economic Impact:** Especially for public figures, or those reliant on public approval, brave expression can sometimes lead to boycotts or loss of business.
- **Psychological Pressure:** The pressure to maintain a brave front after taking a stand can be psychologically demanding and exhausting.

Now, let's put this into action. Take a moment to consider the afore-mentioned risks and rewards. How do they apply to your life? Jot down your thoughts. For each risk, think about a situation where you might face it. How would you handle it? For each reward, envision a scenario where you achieve it. How would that feel?

This exercise is to prepare you for real-life situations where your maverick voice will need to be activated. By knowing what's at stake and what you could gain, you're equipping yourself to make bold choices that are right for you. This is your chance to map out your path to brave expression. Think of it as plotting your course on a treasure map, where each risk is a challenge to overcome and every reward a treasure to be found. As you can see, this path is not for the half-hearted. You will need to back up your words and take responsibility for them, no matter what.

NOT ALL RISKS ARE CREATED EQUAL

Every risk you take in speaking out is as unique as your fingerprint. Your values, your life story—they all play a part in shaping the challenges and chances you'll encounter when you share your thoughts with the world, be it privately or publicly.

Not every thought needs a *billboard* and not every belief requires a *public* parade. You don't have to broadcast every single opinion you have. Don't view this as hiding who you are; experience it as picking the right time and place for your words—that discernment we've been talking about since the start. Taking the leap into honest communication isn't limited to public proclamations or social media posts. It exists in those heart-to-heart conversations you've been avoiding, the ones that happen away from any audience but can shift the ground beneath you. It's perfectly acceptable to have views that you share only in certain spaces or with certain people. Some thoughts are just for you or for close conversations with friends and family.

Not every thought
needs a *billboard* and
not every belief requires
a *public* parade.

Remember, being brave with your words is all a practice in balance. I'll keep saying it because it matters. You've got to know who you are, think about what might happen because of what you say, and have a game plan for how you're going to say it.

Whether you're gearing up for a delicate private conversation or preparing to share your convictions with the world, let the following step-by-step exercise—Your Personalized Risk Framework—be your guide. I first created it for personal use, then started to share it with my clients, and now *you* also have the chance to make it work for you. You will walk away from this exercise trusting that the maverick we spoke about in the previous chapter is ready to be expressed in a considered way.

YOUR PERSONALIZED RISK FRAMEWORK

Topic Identification
Task: Choose three subjects that are stirring within you, whether they're ripe for public sharing or need to be addressed in private settings. It could be a conversation you need to have or topics or issues that really matter to you—the ones you feel a strong urge to speak up about.

Reflection: Why do these subjects press on your heart? What values or experiences are driving you to think about them? (Refer back to Chapter 6.)

Comfort-Level Assessment
Task: Rate how at ease you feel about speaking on each topic, from 1 (really uncomfortable) to 10 (totally at ease).

Reflection: What's behind your comfort level? Is it the emotional weight, potential conflict, or the vulnerability required? Are there

---

gaps in your knowledge, worries about negative feedback, or other personal experiences shaping this?

Benefit Analysis

Task: Think of the best-case scenario for addressing each topic. This might be healing in a personal relationship, progress in self-understanding, personal satisfaction, influencing others, or sparking a dialogue that matters.

Reflection: How do these potential positives feed into your bigger life goals or vision?

Risk Consideration

Task: Acknowledge the potential fallout or challenges for each subject. Consider the impacts on your relationships, mental peace, professional risks, or social standing.

Reflection: Which risks are manageable for you? Are there some that you feel are too high? Which ones might need a careful approach or additional support?

Tactical Strategy Development

Task: Create action plans for each subject that balance your comfort levels and the desired outcomes. This is where you minimize the risks you've identified.
  This might involve:
- Refining the way you present your ideas by preparing for conversations with empathy and research.
- Choosing the right time and place for a private discussion or, if it's public, making sure you're using the platform that will hold your message best (podcasts or blogs are good long-form options, instead of defaulting to the limitations of social media).

- Building a support network that can offer guidance and support—this could be friends, family, or groups who are open-minded and can offer support.

Reflection: How do these strategies equip you to speak up with more assurance?

Now, with your framework in place, you're better positioned to step into discussions with a blend of boldness and prudence. As you engage:

- **Stay Adaptable:** Life is dynamic, so be ready to reevaluate and tweak your framework as you gain new insights and experiences.
- **Seek Feedback:** Have conversations with people you trust to ensure your communication style stays true to you and effective for your audience. Let them help you fine-tune your approach.
- **Practice Resilience:** Difficult conversations are growth opportunities in disguise. Not every conversation will go as planned. Each one can strengthen your framework and your resolve. Use these moments to learn and refine your approach.

This goes beyond just speaking up; it's about connecting with others and getting to know yourself on a deeper level. It doesn't matter if you're opening up to one person or a whole crowd—the stakes are always there, and it takes guts either way. So go ahead and take that step. Your voice counts, both out loud for everyone to hear and in those intimate moments when it's just you and someone else.

In the next chapter, you will be stepping into the arena, a place where imperfect action thrives. It's your move to make. Or rather, the dive is yours to take. Sure, taking that step can be risky, but what you could gain—a real sense of why you're here, making a difference and being in integrity with yourself—is worth reaching for. So take a deep breath, gather your bravery, and leap. Let us see the ripples you'll create!

Chapter 12

Enter the Arena

A mind that embraces The Third Perspective is one that under-stands that the only way to *become* brave and assertive is to put yourself in situations where you can find out what you're truly capable of. It's time to lace up your boots and step into the arena.

Here we are, at a pivotal moment in your unfurling. You've been walking with me through the twists and turns of rediscovering the many layers of your voice, understanding the risks, and mustering the audacity to let people witness who you truly are. Now, it's time for action. Imperfect action. Taking that essential step into the practice ground will be your biggest undertaking. And you'll make the effort even when you're not 100 percent sure, even when your voice trembles. *Especially* when your voice trembles. I'll start by making something clear: mindfulness in how you express yourself is important—I'm not knocking that—but there's a fine line between being *mindful* about what you say, and using mindfulness as an *excuse* to sit on the sidelines.

Perhaps your mind is once again entertaining thoughts like, "I'll wait until I've got it all figured out, until I'm certain I'll say it perfectly." But here's the thing: waiting for the perfect moment or the flawless plan is often a sneaky way of hiding. It's another form of restricting and censoring yourself, a subtle stalling tactic. It's like waiting for a train at an abandoned station—*it's just not coming*. The arena isn't reserved for the flawless; it's *built* for the brave. And bravery doesn't require perfection; but it does mean you show the fuck up, scars, jitters, and all.

Think back to the maverick mindset we talked about in Chapter 10. You're diving in and learning as you go, making waves and not stopping at dipping your toes in the water. It's that deep-down drive that calls you to speak up, to share your story, to offer that idea that's been simmering in the back of your mind.

And let's acknowledge something big here: you are not the same person who first opened this book. With every chapter, every exercise, every moment of introspection, you've been changing. Whether you realize it, feel it, or not. You've been stretching and growing, challenging the boundaries of your old self. The person ready to step into the arena now has a toolkit brimming with strategies, a heart fortified by understanding, and a spark of the maverick ready to burn bright.

So, what does entering the arena look like for you? It's the act of taking the thoughts and ideas that have been swirling around in your head as you've been reading and giving them some air. Now you need to put it all into action. Now it's time to have those conversations you've been avoiding, write that blog post you've been putting off, or be done with the "tweaking" and share your art with the world. Stop hiding in plain sight!

You will stumble. You will fall. It's all part of it—an important part if you ask me! What you're not going to put up with is letting the fear of those stumbles keep you from even trying. I'm amused by how our protective brains will stop us from doing something because we're not yet perfect at it, but how will you become good (forget perfect!) if you won't even step forward and give it a good go? The conditions will never be perfect. Let that knowledge offer you some relief. That maverick inside you? It's itching for a chance to show what it can do. Give it that chance. Let it out. Let it make some damn noise. Let it make a mess. Because that's where the growth happens—in the messy, noisy, *imperfect action*.

There's a fine line between being *mindful* about what you say and using mindfulness as an *excuse* to sit on the sidelines.

STEPPING INTO THE ARENA

Now, let's put all this into a real-life scenario. You've been walking with me through the theory, through the exercises, and you've seen what it takes to be a maverick. But what does it mean when it's your turn to speak, and the room expects you to fall in line with the common opinion?

Imagine you're at a cozy dinner gathering with friends. Laughter floats in the air, mingled with the delicious scent of home-cooked food. Suddenly, a hot topic lands on the table: vaccines. The conversation takes a sharp turn as opinions start flying like dinner rolls in a food fight. You've been dodging this topic, but now it's staring you right in the face. Are you for or against? This false binary becomes a side dish, and your friend, the self-appointed devil's advocate, can't hide his grin. He knows this conversation will churn the waters—his favorite pastime.

Your friends are diving in, each sharing their stance, and you know your view doesn't quite match up with theirs. As the conversation swirls to you, your stomach tightens. You're silently wishing the earth would swallow you up. You're at the table, fork in hand, decision time ticking away. What's the plan? What do you do now? You're not looking to win a debate trophy; you're aiming to share your piece without losing your peace. It's about choosing when to speak up and when to listen, when to engage and when to sit back and enjoy your lasagna.

You decide to lean into that maverick mindset. You remember that opting out of a black-or-white answer isn't giving up—it's choosing your path. You acknowledge the chaos of human conversation and, with a cool head, you assess how to best contribute. This isn't about shying away; it's about choosing your moment with the wisdom of all you've learned. In this charged dinner scenario, embracing your inner maverick means speaking your truth, even if it's unconventional. Remember, you've been preparing for moments like these. You might

That's where the growth happens—in the messy, noisy, *imperfect action*.

take a deep breath and say, "Actually, I've chosen not to get vaccinated. Sure, I respect the science and the decisions others have made, but for me, it's about weighing up personal health concerns and values. I think it's key we have open, nonjudgmental discussions about these choices, as they're deeply personal and more complex than we make them out to be." This response boldly shares your perspective, acknowledges the multifaceted nature of the issue, and invites understanding rather than conflict.

But what if the room doesn't let up? Perhaps you, the reader, are already finding yourself picking sides as you take in this scenario— notice this, stay in the role of "witness," and continue on. If someone at the table retorts, "But don't you think that by not getting vaccinated, you're putting others at risk? It's not just about personal choice—it's a public health issue. There's a lot of misinformation out there, and it worries me that intelligent people are falling for these anti-vax arguments. Don't you think it's a bit irresponsible?"—this is when your boundary setting comes into play.

Your voice, like any muscle, grows stronger with use. This is your chance to use it. You've gained confidence and tools from your journey through these pages. So, when the conversation circles back to you, you're ready. This isn't just about vaccines or dinner debates; it's about every situation where you have the chance to be heard or choose your words wisely.

Now, it's time to practice reflection instead of deflection; when faced with criticism, consider its merit before responding. You might say, "I appreciate your interest in my take, but I'd rather not delve into specifics right now. All I have to say is that I believe we all have to make the choices that are right for us." A statement like this is assertive yet respectful, marking your boundaries without shutting the conversation down. Focus on controlling what you can—your tone, your body language, and the energy with which you deliver your boundary. Remember, defensiveness doesn't have to be your go-to reaction.

It's important to note that, in this scenario, refusing to turn it into a pro versus anti debate isn't self-censorship. It's exercising discernment, the wisdom to manage your inner world and navigate social situations with respect for yourself and others. This incident at the dinner table is a clear demonstration of this. You didn't censor your thoughts out of fear of being judged or isolated. Instead, you just felt that getting into a deeper discussion about it in that moment might not be helpful. You respected the moment and everyone's different thoughts, without forcing yourself to speak.

As you can see, unleashing your newfound boldness requires accepting that you're going to run into some challenging situations. I have more strategies ready to help you move through these tricky interactions with finesse and courage.

NAVIGATING TRICKY INTERACTIONS

Your maverick muscles are getting a workout. When you're in the heat of the moment and people are expecting an opinion from you, it's easy to imagine doomsday scenarios, to think that one slipup could cost you friendships or respect. But is it really that dire? Will the world tilt on its axis based on what you say next? Probably not. This is your chance to see beyond the black and white, to explore the nuanced space where your true voice lives—The Third Perspective. You have several choices you can make, given you can keep your cool. Can you step back and see all the different options that could lead you to the same goal?

THE POWER OF THE PAUSE

During a charged conversation, it can be hard to find a moment to gather your thoughts or step back from the discussion. You feel the familiar rush of adrenaline, that fight-or-flight instinct kicking in. The "fight" part means you might feel defensive, ready to confront the issue head-on, like standing your ground in an argument. The "flight" part means you might feel like avoiding the problem, like leaving a challenging conversation. Maybe there's a temptation to smooth things over, to nod along just to avoid a fuss—that's the lesser-known "fawn" response. It's something we've all done. I found out about this response a few years ago, and suddenly a lot of my past behaviors made sense. This is when, instead of fighting or fleeing, you try to please or appease others to defuse tension or, again, avoid conflict. You might find yourself agreeing just to keep the peace, even if you don't truly feel that way. In these moments, it's easy to act without thinking. But now's the time to realize that there's power in the pause. Use the pause strategically. It's a moment of power that allows you to collect your thoughts and respond rather than react. In that moment of silence, you can also remember that every person has their story, just like you do.

BOUNDARIES WITHOUT DEFENSIVENESS

As you enter the arena of real-world interactions, a key skill to master is the art of setting boundaries and doing so in a way that's firm but not defensive. The goal isn't to cut off conversations or build barriers between yourself and others. I say this because I find that our mainstream dialogue around boundaries can be quite cutthroat, as it gives a sense of "My way or the highway!"—that's not what we're talking about here. It's more about understanding and respecting your own limits—how much you're able to handle emotionally and intellectually at any given moment.

Think back to the values we've talked about and the decision you made about how much risk you're willing to take in your conversations. This kind of self-awareness is vital for setting boundaries effectively. In conversations, especially the tough ones, being clear on what you can and can't handle is essential. This clarity can only come from a deep understanding of your values and your comfort level with risk.

For example, if a conversation starts to go against your core values or gets too intense for you, knowing how to bring it back on track or exit gracefully shows how aware you are of yourself and how dedicated you are to your principles.

Here are some nuanced ways to handle these moments:

- **Request for Reflection:** Sometimes, all you need is a brief moment to absorb what's being said. Saying, "Give me a moment to process this" can be a game changer. I do this all the time. It not only allows you to process what's been said, but subtly breaks the rhythm of an intense exchange. When emotions run high, that little step back can be invaluable because it helps you digest, while signaling to others your intention to understand.

- **Intent to Ponder:** If you feel the subject demands more contemplation, consider expressing your intent to think more deeply. In a world that demands instant reactions, you can choose to *respond* differently. Try saying, "I need some time to really think about this before I respond. Can I get back to you?" or "This is a complex topic, and I want to give it the thought it deserves. Can we revisit this later?" It signals respect for the conversation and its depth.

- **No Opinion, No Pressure:** There's no rule that says you must have an opinion on everything. A simple "At the moment, I don't have much to contribute to this discussion" lifts the weight off your shoulders. In a culture that expects an opinion on everything, admitting you don't know can be refreshing. If you're still forming your thoughts, or if the subject is outside your area of knowledge or interest, saying "I don't have enough information to have a strong opinion on this" keeps you true to yourself. It can be honest and freeing.

Each small win, each act of *bravery*—no matter how minor it seems—is a step toward greater *confidence*.

- **Hit the Pause Button:** If the conversation becomes too heated or confrontational, phrases like "I need a moment to gather my thoughts. Can we pause?" or "This is important, but I can't discuss it right now. Can we talk later?" or "Let's pause for a second, I think we're getting off track" allow you to take control of the situation and set a boundary—plus it helps in maintaining a constructive dialogue.

- **Ask to Slow the Pace:** If a conversation's pace is too much, you can slow things down and give yourself room to breathe with "I value what you're sharing, but I'm feeling overwhelmed. Can we take this a bit slower?" This allows for a more digestible pace of exchange. I personally find it especially useful to turn to this strategy when I'm having a challenging conversation with a romantic partner or family member.

- **Reschedule Entirely:** If you find yourself too scattered to contribute meaningfully, suggesting a later time can be beneficial. "My thoughts are a bit jumbled right now; I'm not in the right headspace to continue. Would it be okay if we picked up this conversation another time?" is a considerate way to reset. It shows that you respect both the discussion and your well-being equally.

As you continue to practice asserting yourself and remaining open in conversations, you will need to remember to ditch the script. Life isn't a scripted play. The guidance and prompts in this book are merely starting points, tools to help build your confidence and refine your approach. In your day-to-day interactions, you'll no doubt meet people whose beliefs and values differ markedly from yours. Their perspectives will challenge you, and their decision-making processes may seem foreign. This is where the real practice happens, in the thick of diverse, face-to-face interactions. Be ready to improvise, adapt, and speak from the heart, while remaining open to the reality of multiple perspectives and truths. You will also need to celebrate those small victories! Each small win, each act of *bravery*—no matter how minor it seems—is a step toward greater *confidence*.

THE WORLD OF ONLINE EXPRESSION

Now, a word of caution: social media should not be the first arena where you test out your bold new voice. It might be the go-to for some, but most people throw themselves into it prematurely without building a steady ground offline—then they inevitably find themselves feeling ungrounded and far too vulnerable. I repeat: **DO NOT MAKE SOCIAL MEDIA YOUR TESTING GROUND**. Why? Because as we've covered, it's the Wild West. The dynamics of digital platforms are very different from in-person interactions. Online, emotions get cranked up to 11, and the subtle shades of conversation often get lost in the digital noise.

Your real-life, face-to-face interactions? That's where you get to really see how people react, sense their emotions, and fine-tune your approach on the fly. These skills? They're gold, and they're what you need to master first. It's in these interpersonal exchanges where the best practice happens. So, before you leap onto the social media stage to show off your newfound courage, start with the people right in front of you. Practice in the real world, where conversations are rich and the learning is deep. This is your actual training ground—one you have access to even in those micro-moments.

As you grow more comfortable and skilled in expressing yourself boldly and listening deeply in person, you'll be better prepared to handle the world of online expression. Think of it like this: you're building a solid foundation of real-world confidence and skill in the real world before stepping into the digital arena with full force, and you have more than enough tools and exercises that will help you step into your digital persona in other courageous ways. I can't say it enough: the path to brave expression is a marathon, not a sprint. Take it one step at a time, and watch closely as your confidence and impact grow.

AN AUDACIOUS REINTRODUCTION

There comes a moment in life when you stand at the crossroads of change, looking back at the person you were and ahead to the person you're about to become. Imagine walking into a room where everyone knows your old story, the one where you've promised to quit drinking again and again. I've been there, done that—more times than I care to admit. As you now know, one of the most pivotal crossroads for me was when I decided, for what felt like the umpteenth time, to give sobriety another chance. Except, this wasn't simply another attempt; it ended up being an audacious reintroduction to myself and the world.

You see, reintroducing yourself isn't about changing an aspect of your life. It's about acknowledging that a full-bodied change has to take place, and it's already been stirring within you. It's about having the courage to accept that sometimes you have to let go of the *familiar* narrative, even if it means stepping away from the comfort of long-held personas and communities. This is where entering the arena takes on a whole new meaning. And yes, you will have to confront the possibility that not everyone will welcome the new you with open arms (this is where your self-reputation matters most— see Chapter 9).

When I made my choice, I had to come to terms with the reality that my "party friends" might no longer find my presence valuable if I wasn't knocking one back with them, or they might see my decision as me saying I'm better than them. You'd be surprised how often this happens to people. It was a stark realization that, by changing, I was also altering the dynamics of these relationships,

Sometimes you have to let
go of the *familiar* narrative,
even if it means stepping
away from the comfort
of long-held personas
and communities.

including some that had been in place for nearly a decade. It all had to crumble to the ground so I could rebuild. But the most profound peace came from accepting that my life, as I knew it, was ripe for metamorphosis.

Reintroducing yourself to *yourself* is going to be the most challenging yet rewarding part of this whole thing. Why? Because you may have a fixed idea about who you are and what you're capable of, and, naturally, it will take a period of practice and adjustment to get acquainted with the version of you that operates a little bit (or a lot) differently—that maverick you've been cultivating since Chapter 10. And guess what? You already have the blueprint for it. It's been carved into your being through every experience, every reflection, every lesson learned.

The process of shedding layers—whether they're beliefs you've outgrown, fears that once held you back, or ideologies that no longer serve you—is like stepping out of an old skin. Each brave act I've ever taken in my life always turned out to be more than a declaration; it was an act of liberation. Thinking back to my rejection of victimhood, I can see that I was tired of the act, tired of people telling me how I should think or feel because of my race. I was over it. And that meant it was time to clean house. The fear of being misunderstood had kept my voice in chains for far too long, but the decision to face it head-on was a choice to unshackle myself and reclaim my narrative. I also wanted to make it known that my views had changed. I was no longer willing to be a performer or a puppet. I was taking my story back.

And now, I turn to you. Our work together through the pages of this book has given you insight into the theory behind brave expression. That's great! But the true test lies in the practice—in the doing. It's in the active steps you take to embody this new phase of your communication and identity. You've been preparing for this, perhaps without even realizing it, every time you chose to speak up, to question, or to express something that didn't quite fit the mold.

Now, it's time to take a deliberate step toward reintroduction. You'll piece together the evidence of your past—those moments, big and small, where you've already begun the process of redefining who you are. You can't just talk yourself into an evolution; you must live it, breathe it, and embody it. BE it.

As you stand poised to reintroduce yourself, think about this for a moment: What does your blueprint look like? What evidence in your past can show you that you've already reintroduced yourself before? Many times, I'm sure. You just didn't know that this is what was taking place. Perhaps you're convincing yourself that no grand revelation is necessary. But ask yourself, is that the whole truth?

As you work through the following exercise, I want you to remember that each step away from old beliefs and toward new understanding is a courageous act of self-redefinition. Your past is extremely rich with these moments. By reflecting on these steps, you'll not only see the road map you've been crafting all along, but also gain the clarity and confidence needed for your next audacious reintroduction. Grand gestures are not necessary, but you will need to align the outside world with your internal growth. You will need to be fearless in your evolution and fully own the maverick within you.

TRACING YOUR IDEOLOGICAL EVOLUTION

As we venture into this exercise, I'll kick things off by sharing my personal experiences as a guide. There have been key moments in my life when I've needed to take a step back and critically reassess the ideas I used to be all-in on. These were beliefs that I thought defined who I was, but over time, they started making me feel self-righteous, dimming my ability for compassion and critical thinking. And this got in the way of seeing things from other people's point of view. Chances are, you've been at similar crossroads too—moments when you found the courage to question what you always believed, to let go of old ways of thinking, and to open up to new ideas. Let's walk through these times together, and see how and why our ideologies evolve.

Step 1: Pinpoint Moments of Ideological Shift

Think about the times in your life when you started to wonder if what you believed was right for you. These are the moments when you began to move away from opinions or ideas that you used to agree with, leading to big shifts in how you see things. Identify at least three of these pivotal moments where your ideology evolved or grew in a new direction. Write them down, and think about what caused these changes—was it an event, a conversation, or something else? And how did your worldview change because of it?

Example from My Life: There was a time in my life when I was deeply entrenched in certain social justice beliefs. For instance:

- **Identity Politics:** I used to think the only way to look at *any* social issue was through the lens of race, gender, or cultural identity. I saw these identities as the be-all and end-all for understanding *every* problem in the world.
- **Language Policing:** I was pretty rigid and strict about how people should *talk* about gender, race, and identity. If someone didn't use the exact terms I thought were right, I'd see it as a deeply problematic issue, something really offensive.
- **Zero Tolerance for Microaggressions:** I'd often take offense to things people said or did, thinking of them as microaggressions (them being purposefully discriminatory), without

241

stopping, even for a second, to consider what they really meant or where they were coming from.

Although the previous examples were well-intentioned because they stemmed from a genuine desire for equality and justice, these beliefs began to make me feel superior and dismissive of other people. There was no balance. This way of thinking made me see the world in a very black-and-white way and often put me at odds with people who didn't see things *exactly* as I did. Recognizing this, I made a conscious decision to step away, confront my biases, actively listen, and consider views that didn't mirror my own. I needed to make space to understand where others were coming from. I needed to have those strongly held beliefs tested to see if they really held up.

Step 2: Internal Shifts and Growth

For each moment you made a note of, delve into the internal shift that prompted your change. What realizations did you have? How did this shift in perspective change how you saw yourself?

Example from My Life: I realized that my previous beliefs were closing me off from connecting with others. In fact, I had been pushing people away without realizing. As I moved away from that rigid state of mind, I found myself becoming more understanding and less judgmental. Of myself, and of other people.

Step 3: Reactions and Support Systems

Reflect on the responses you received from those around you during your transition. Who offered support and who was resistant? Consider how you managed these reactions and what they taught you about resilience and self-awareness.

Example from My Life: When I shared my new outlook (which I did behind the scenes before announcing it publicly to my audience and clients), some friends were puzzled and didn't quite understand to begin with; most were intrigued. I learned to navigate these reactions with patience, seeing each as an opportunity for continuing the conversation.

Step 4: Declaring Your New Perspective

Consider how you communicated this ideological evolution to your circle. Did you find yourself having deeper conversations, writing about your experiences, or perhaps showing through your actions that you were embracing a new way of thinking?

Example from My Life: I began to engage in conversations that bridged divides, which became my main goal—and further down the line it became a big part of the work I do today: finding common ground in an increasingly divided world. I shared and engaged with teachings that reflected a wide range of views and invited discussions that I would have previously avoided like the plague.

Step 5: Unveiling Your Blueprint

Identify the core traits that revealed themselves each time you shifted your perspective. This is your blueprint—your underlying framework that has guided you through each reintroduction to new ways of thinking and being.

Example from My Life: At the heart of my ideological shifts was a desire for authenticity and a need to understand the world in its full complexity, beyond the confines of any single belief system.

Step 6: Envisioning Your Evolved Self

Imagine how you would introduce your current self, with all the growth and changes in beliefs, to someone from your past. What would you say? How would you articulate the richness and depth that this evolution has brought to your life?

Example from My Life: I've allowed myself to experience many beliefs, and each one has taught me something valuable. And today, I choose to continue being open-minded and ready to learn. While still standing for something!

Step 7: Living Out Loud

Choose an action that signifies your commitment to this new, open-minded self. Make it an action that resonates with your core values and reflects your growth.

Example from My Life: I decided to start a limited series podcast that explored some controversial topics through the lens of restorative justice and it became a space for diverse, respectful discussions. Conversations I never imagined I would have, let alone publicly!

Remember, this exercise isn't a one-off task. It's a powerful tool you can return to any time you feel at the crossroads of change. You've done it before, you can do it again. With each choice, each word, each interaction, you are unfolding a new chapter of your existence. You're shedding layers, and allowing yourself to start again—what a freeing and open way to view life.

If you're still with me, walking the path that my words have carved, you've earned my deepest respect. That's because I know the truth:

when the real work starts, many people step back but not you. You've understood that this book is more than just words; it's a call to action. These pages are a starting point, not an end. The real renewal begins when you weave these lessons and tools into the very fabric of your everyday life. That's how you truly reintroduce yourself: to yourself, to those around you, and to the world at large. Welcome to your Third Perspective.

Final Note

Every groundbreaking discovery in history, every transformative revolution, every thought-provoking piece of art was born in a mind that dared to venture beyond "the box"—the societal norms, the accepted standards, the conventional ways of thinking. The minds that we most admire in human history embraced *rebellious thoughts*, questioned the status quo, and didn't cower in fear of being seen as "problematic." They weren't just thinking outside the box; they were acting as if the box didn't exist at all.

Someone who dared to think beyond the societal norms of her time is the extraordinary Mbuya Nehanda. As a spiritual leader of the Shona people, the tribe I come from, she was a major inspiration for the First Chimurenga/Umvukela, the uprising against British colonists in present-day Zimbabwe in the late nineteenth century.

A woman in a deeply patriarchal society, Nehanda did not let gender stereotypes restrict her thinking or actions. Her role as a medium gave her status among her people. She used this platform to inspire and mobilize them against the oppressive colonial regime. Her famous words, "My bones will rise again," became a rallying cry for future generations seeking liberation.

When she was captured by the colonial forces and sentenced to death, Nehanda refused to submit. She remained defiant, not displaying fear or remorse, which further cemented her status as a symbol of resistance.

Nehanda's bold and nonconformist thinking challenged the prevailing power structures of her time. The fear of retribution or societal expectations, and even death, were not enough to silence her voice. Her legacy remains a potent symbol of resistance and empowerment in my home of Zimbabwe, and beyond. In the face of adversity, she personifies the idea of thinking like there is no box. Her actions and fearlessness had far-reaching implications, inspiring future generations to continue the struggle for independence.

Reflecting on my own life, especially as a Zimbabwean woman from the Shona tribe, I find that Nehanda's resilience and fearlessness hold a profound significance for me. The very essence of this book has been to push you beyond your perceived limitations, to see beyond societal constraints, and to embrace the audacity of your expression. While I might now be miles away from the soils of Zimbabwe, Nehanda's legacy is a compass that guides me through every twist and turn of my narrative. Her legacy has guided me in writing this book.

Being an immigrant in the United Kingdom, one who doesn't think in the way that's expected, I sometimes confront moments when I'm tempted to dilute my voice, to meld with the majority, or to avoid ruffling feathers. Each time that trepidation creeps in, I'm reminded of Nehanda's unwavering spirit. It makes me think, if she could be brave back then, shouldn't I also have the courage to speak up and stand for what I believe, especially with the freedoms I have today?

Throughout this book, we've talked about being open-minded, believing in ourselves, rethinking our views, and knowing our limits. These principles are not simply abstract concepts. They're embodied in the lived experiences of trailblazers like Nehanda. She was the epitome of someone who understood her limitations yet pushed against them with a force that will resonate for generations to come.

The minds that we most admire in human history embraced *rebellious thoughts*, questioned the status quo, and didn't cower in fear of being seen as "problematic."

Whenever I face daunting situations or feel the weight of internal and external pressure, I often close my eyes and envision Nehanda standing behind me (I find visualization to be a very powerful tool!). I imagine her seasoned hands—those very hands that once defied an empire—resting on my shoulders, lending me a fragment of her invincible spirit. In her whispers, I hear words of encouragement, pushing me to go further, to speak louder, and to walk paths others might avoid.

Because of Nehanda, and countless others who've paved the way, I have the privilege to live a life unburdened by the constant shadow of fear. It's a responsibility I don't take lightly. Each time I share my thoughts, voice my opinions, or simply exist authentically in spaces where I once felt out of place, I'm honoring her legacy. I'm ensuring that her sacrifice, her courage, was not in vain.

No matter your origin or background, I hope that you too find your "Nehanda"—that guiding spirit who reminds you of the shoulders you stand on, urging you to reach for heights unimagined. Remember that when you choose to think as if there's no box, you are not just pushing back against societal expectations. You're honoring every courageous heart that imagined a limitless world.

Thinking outside the box is not restricted to being opinionated for the sake of it. It's being nonnegotiably true to yourself, standing up for what you believe in, and using your unique voice to effect change—including when it's uncomfortable or inconvenient.

Your thoughts will invite criticism. Your ideas will push buttons; they might even make you feel uncomfortable. But that's exactly what makes them valuable. These are the thoughts that provoke conversations, that disrupt complacency, that inspire change.

I'm not saying we all need to act as revolutionaries. We don't all need to lead big changes or fight against the system every day. That's tough work and not for everyone. Some people thrive on challenging everything and facing conflict head-on. But what I do suggest is that we open our minds a bit more. I am saying we must open up a revolutionary dimension in our mind. A place to consider what those around you ignore. A place to allow new ideas to build. A place where you can practice saying, "I disagree with you. I've been thinking along different lines," and then accept the consequences of speaking up.

As we reach the end of our time together (although in many ways it's only the beginning), take a moment to reflect on how the three pillars—Awareness, Responsibility, and Expression—have prepared you to swim the often-divisive waters of today's world. The tools and insights you've collected here are more than strategies; they will be your compass in times when societal currents urge you to pick a side. Focusing on all that is happening outside of you can be a surefire way to find yourself in a constant state of disempowerment and hopelessness, which is why the goal of this book was to help you redirect your energy and focus on what you can control. Yes, be aware of what you *can't* control, but give your time and attention to what you *can*. If you stay committed to taking practical action, you are going to witness your mind, your voice, your entire *being* becoming stronger with each day that passes. It will take time. It will take repeated efforts on your part. But it will liberate you in ways that will blow your entire mind. You've learned the difference between muting your voice out of fear and thoughtfully selecting your words; now you'll use these skills to guide you as you walk that fine line with grace and assurance. And you'll do so with both confidence *and* empathy.

You stand with a clearer understanding of your belief system, and you're armed with the knowledge that you have the power to rewrite your story at any point. Even if you get it wrong, feel like you've regressed, or fucked up in some way, you're going to get back up and

In a world that's quick to "cancel," be brave enough to explore the limitless layers of your expression, dare to question, and *think freely*.

stay the course! Your values, now refined and clarified, will be the torch that lights the way, particularly in moments that challenge your comfort and convictions. The maverick within you, now awakened, leads the charge with a style of communication that prioritizes genuine connections and a healthy curiosity. Think like there is no box, but do so with the intention of creating understanding, not division; of sparking dialogue, not discord; of challenging norms, not disrespecting them. In doing so, you not only allow yourself the freedom to think creatively, but you also create a space where others feel safe to do the same.

In a world that's quick to "cancel," be brave enough to explore the limitless layers of your expression, dare to question, to *think freely*. Be bold enough to become an embodiment of The Third Perspective. The box doesn't exist, unless you create it. You only limit yourself if you decide to. As you close this book and prepare for the rest of your adventure, carry these insights with you. The maverick within you is no longer a concept; it's a living, breathing part of who you are, ready to engage with the world in meaningful, impactful ways. Your voice, now more than ever, is crucial to our collective narrative. Step out with confidence, curiosity, and a commitment to being authentically you. The world awaits the unique imprint of your thoughts, words, and actions—your brave expression. I'll see you on the other side of conformity!

Acknowledgments

The gratitude is pouring out of me. I must start off with a special, full-bodied thank-you to **my clients, my audience, my supporters, and every single person I've met along the way** who's inspired and encouraged me to continue speaking and to continue listening. You keep me sane and, most of all, you keep me brave. This book can only exist out there in the world because of you, and that's not something I take lightly. My promise to you is to never take the connection we have for granted.

Ivan Mulcahy—My agent. My Special Friend Behind the Hedge. I'm tearing up as I write these words because without you, well… let's not think about that. Since I was a little girl, I always knew that one day I would write a book, and despite being approached by at least a dozen editors and publishers over the course of my career, not once did I feel the alignment I needed to say YES. All of that changed when I received your encouraging, refreshing, and provoking email at the top of 2021. You had read my open letter, it shifted something within you, but you knew there was so much more to my story than those four thousand words. And you were right. You didn't pigeonhole me; you gave me the space and time to step fully into my wisdom and allowed me to see that there was something special here. You are more than my agent (a damn good one at that!); you have become a dear friend and someone I consider family. You understand my voice, my heart, my being—and how lucky are we that we both have a love for dark, and often crude, humor. Which adds layers of sophistication, mischief, and FUN into our work. You are my second voice, my second brain, and someone I'll be creating magic with, for all eternity!

Lauren Whelan—You are magic personified. There are some people who come into your life, and you immediately know that this is someone you'll be in companionship with for years to come. You are that person for me. As my publisher and now friend, you have made this entire process worthwhile. Not only that, you have also given me the push I needed to become a better writer. In moments when I felt like pulling the plug, I always knew that I could rely on you to bring me back to earth. A deep bow to you and my team at Hachette/Hodder Catalyst, particularly **Oliver Malcolm**, who spent a good couple of years chasing me because he knew that this book was going to be transformational—way before it existed! Oli, thank you for being persistent, encouraging me to stay audacious, and having my back throughout.

Becca Mundy and **Alice Morley**—Thank you for thinking like there is no box and doing everything in your power to get this book into as many hands as possible. My creative vision, along with the level of ambition I had, could not have been fulfilled without you.

Julia Kellaway—My goodness, where do I even begin? I hope you're wearing a smile on your face as you take in these words because you are an absolute joy. You saved me in more ways than you'll ever know. From the very first day we started working together, I knew that you were the perfect person to walk alongside me as I wrote the book I've always dreamed of writing. Accepting your edits over and over again was a pleasure because you *always* got it right. You are another person who truly understands and *hears* the nuances of my voice, which means you can call me on it when I'm holding back. You are not only an editing genius and a sharp strategist, you're one of the most grounded, hilarious, and thoughtful people I've come across.

Thank you for seeing just how powerful this book would be, especially in the moments when I couldn't.

Luke Bird—As someone who is taken by all things Beauty (me), I'm truly grateful that you were the first designer my tasteful editor Lauren brought forward, and we ended up being a great match. Luke, you created a cover that perfectly represents what The Third Perspective is. From our first call together, you immediately understood the vision, and the execution exceeded all expectations I had. Thank you. Our next one will be even better.

Lisa Gallagher—As my agent and beacon of calm from across the pond, your unwavering support and commitment has been invaluable. Even through the rough patches, your fierce belief in me, our team, and the mission of this book remained a guiding force. Thank you for always reassuring me that everything would unfold exactly as it should. As I expected, you were right.

Lauren Marino—I can't thank you enough for pushing me to operate at my very best, for challenging me to think deeply about my "why," and for encouraging me to keep the rawness in my voice. My gratitude also flows to the rest of the team at Hachette US who made me feel heard and appreciated, even when I slightly went against the way they were used to doing things. You made sure my vision was honored nonetheless.

Mary Ann Naples—From the first meeting we had, you got it. You saw the magic of *The Third Perspective*, and you affirmed my voice in ways I truly needed at the time in ways I will never forget. You didn't just believe in what I had to say, you also trusted me completely with the creative reins. Thank you for honoring the fullness of my voice and for being part of one of the greatest undertakings of my life.

Rich Seaman—I hope you get a chance to read these words because you are one of the most glorious and inspiring men I've had the pleasure of knowing and loving. Thank you for caring for me so deeply, stroking and kissing my head, making me cups of tea, and cheering me on while I gave life to this book. A memory I'll treasure forever is standing in that little bookstore in Harpenden, cuddling with you in the Philosophy section as you helped me decide what the subtitle of this book was going to be. Do you remember how excited we both were when we landed on it? I'll love you for as long as I live.

Roxanne Ivy—My creative muse. Since we were teenagers walking the streets of Shepherd's Bush singing Arcade Fire, you've never stopped showing me what it looks and feels like to trust that creativity has no limits. You remind me that I can do anything I put my mind to. From the moment I decided to write this book, you've been with me every step of the way. You appointed yourself as my well-being officer—checking in daily to make sure I'm taking breaks and eating well while in my writing cave. Thank you, Rox.

Thank you to my divine Mama **Jennifer "J-Lo" Muchenje**; my wonderful siblings **Jessie Garande**, **Amanda Garande**, **Elijah Garande**; my family back home in Zimbabwe, all over the African continent, and in the diaspora—you've been my biggest cheerleaders along the way, and there's no better feeling. We've come a long way, huh? **Dwayne, Kunashe, and Chichi**—Aunty loves you! My smart babies. I know how proud you are of me. One day you will read this book and we will talk about what it means to you. Show me off to your friends, will you!

Alewya Demmisse, Fido Fawo, Andrew Odong, Luti Fagbenle, Corina Chercheja, Rui Liu—My dear friends. You have been incredibly generous with your love, mentorship, and support for the collective decades I've known you. There will never be enough words to truly express the appreciation I have for you and our friendship. You, too, are my chosen family. You have all spurred me on, spoken greatness upon me, and reminded me of my gifts at *every* phase of my creative journey—before this book, during it, and after it. You are all embodiments of The Third Perspective; there is absolutely no doubt about that. Thank you for holding me as highly as I hold you. We have big work to do in the world!

About the Author

Africa Brooke is a Zimbabwean born, internationally acclaimed consultant, accredited coach, speaker, and podcaster. As the founder and CEO of Africa Brooke International, she is renowned for her expertise and nuanced insights into overcoming self-sabotage and self-censorship. In these areas she offers specialized consulting and high-level coaching services, along with ongoing support to public figures, teams, and individuals worldwide. Hosting two weekly personal development and philosophy podcasts, *Beyond the Self* and *Unthinkable Thoughts*, Africa's voice has resonated across various media platforms. She has been a sought-after guest on numerous television shows, podcasts, and radio broadcasts. Her contributions to mainstream publications, including *The Guardian*, showcase her thought leadership, and her impactful keynotes have graced the halls of prestigious institutions, including Cambridge University. Africa is based in London.